# THE JAZZ LANGUAGE

## by Dan Haerle

## Table of Contents



© 1980 STUDIO 224
All Rights Assigned to and Controlled by ALFRED PUBLISHING CO., INC.
All Rights Reserved

# INTRODUCTION

The jazz language is a specialized form of communication within the world of music. To be able to express himself fluently, the jazz musician must have a good grasp of the grammar, vocabulary and structures of this language. This simply means that he must have a thorough understanding of the construction of chords and scales and a ready knowledge of their applications as resources which are available to serve his expression.

This book presents all of the materials commonly used by the jazz musician in a logical order dictated both by complexity and need. Some of the materials discussed are more relevant to the needs of a writer and others more useful to an improviser. The book is not intended to be either an arranging or improvisation text but merely a reference providing the information a musician needs to pursue any activity he wishes.

At the end of each chapter is found a set of study questions. These relate directly to the text material of the preceding chapter and serve as either a review guide or as an indicator of one's understanding of the context. Writing, keyboard and ear-training exercises are also included. Obviously, these exercises are relevant to the use of the book as a text for a jazz theory course. However, the student pursuing an understanding of the jazz idiom through individual study should also make use of these exercises.

Students are encouraged to use the piano keyboard as a graphic means of visualizing concepts relating to chord and scale construction. The keyboard exercises provided are intended to give the musician a basic functional use of the piano as a tool. However, the piano should be used in all facets of the growth of either a writer or improviser for solid understanding of harmonic concepts.

# 1. INTERVALS

Intervals are found both in horizontal (melodic) and vertical (harmonic) structures in music. A musician in any idiom of music must be thoroughly grounded in a solid understanding of intervals in the following ways:

1) He must know how to spell (construct) them in any key.
2) He must be able to identify them both visually and aurally when he sees or hears them.
3) He must be able to conceptualize the intervals by singing, either vocally or internally.
4) He must be able to play them anywhere within the range of his instrument.

An interval is simply the distance between two notes. This distance is measured by the number of whole and/or half steps between the two notes involved. Sometimes an interval may be defined as a combination of two smaller intervals. An example of both ways of thinking might be the following: A perfect 5th consists of 3½ steps or is the combination of a major 3rd and a minor 3rd.

Example 1

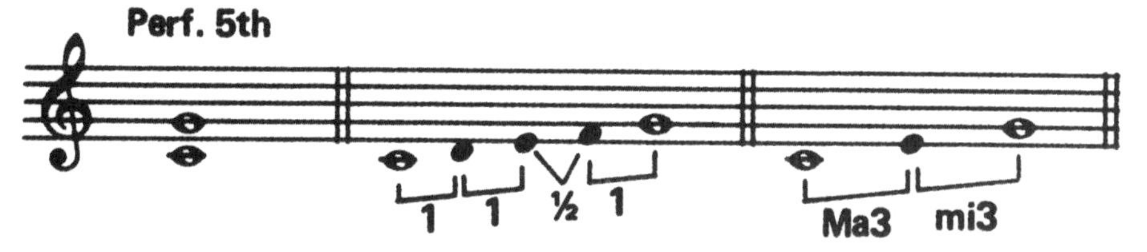


There are basically two kinds of intervals: *melodic* and *harmonic*. Melodic intervals are those which involve two successive tones and harmonic intervals consist of two tones which occur simultaneously.

Example 2

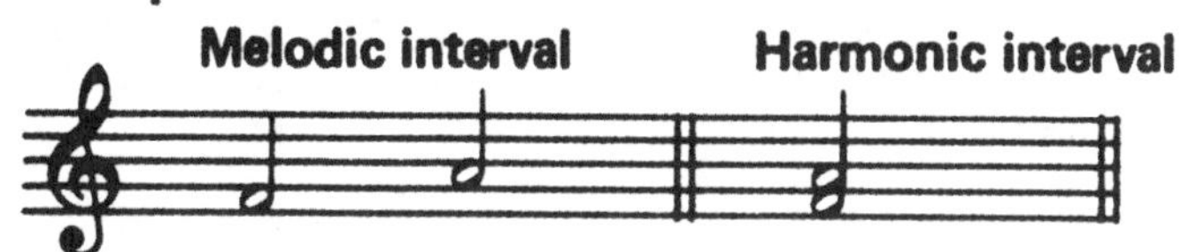


Another way of conceiving intervals is to relate them to some portion of a major or minor scale. For example, a major 3rd is composed of the 1st and 3rd notes of a major scale. A good knowledge of major and minor scales is essential to many kinds of theoretical activity.

Example 3

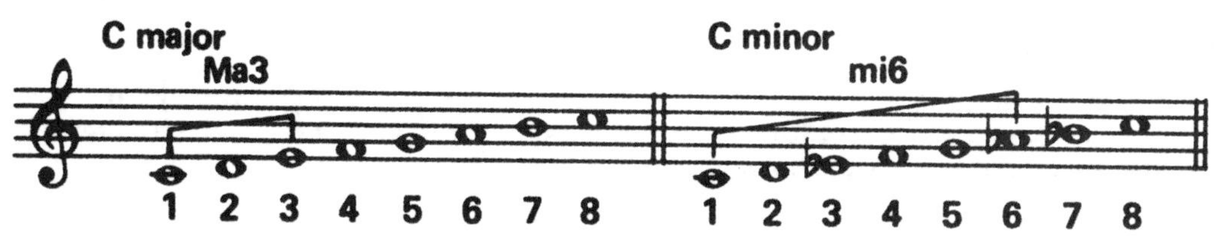


The following chart displays the most common major, minor and perfect intervals. They are discribed in three ways: 1) by the number of whole and/or half steps, 2) by combining two smaller intervals, and 3) by locating them in a major or minor scale.

| INTERVAL | NUMBER OF STEPS | INTERVAL COMBINATION | LOCATION |
|---|---|---|---|
| minor 2nd | ½ step | (none smaller) | closest of all intervals |
| major 2nd | 1 whole step | 2 half steps | 1 & 2, major |
| minor 3rd | 1½ steps | 3 half steps | 1 & 3, minor |
| major 3rd | 2 whole steps | 4 half steps | 1 & 3, major |
| perfect 4th | 2½ steps | maj 3rd and half step, min 3rd and whole step | 1 & 4, major or minor |
| perfect 5th | 3½ steps | maj 3rd and min 3rd, per 4th and whole step | 1 & 5, major or minor |
| minor 6th | 4 whole steps | min 3rd and per 4th, two maj 3rds, per 5th and half step | 1 & 6, minor |
| major 6th | 4½ steps | maj 3rd and per 4th, per 5th and whole step | 1 & 6, major |
| minor 7th | 5 whole steps | min 3rd and per 5th, two per 4ths | 1 & 7, minor |
| major 7th | 5½ steps | per 5th and maj 3rd | 1 & 7, major |
| octave | 6 whole steps | per 5th and per 4th | 1 & 8, major or minor |

A musician should be able to spell intervals correctly and enharmonically. That is, a 3rd should involve two letters a 3rd apart, a 5th should involve two letters a 5th apart, and so on. However, for various musical reasons, intervals are often "mis-spelled" enharmonically with letters that produce the correct sound but are not the correct distance apart. The following example shows both the correct and enharmonic spelling of several intervals.

Example 4

Perf.4 (misspelled) min.6 (misspelled) Ma6 (misspelled)

Technically speaking, an interval which is mis-spelled enharmonically should really be relabeled as another type of interval. The following example shows the correct relabeling of the intervals from Example 4.

Example 5

Perf.4 aug.3 min6 aug.5 Ma6 dim.7

Any of the major, minor or perfect intervals may be *augmented* (increased in size by a half step) or *diminished* (decreased in size by a half step). For example, an augmented 2nd consists of 1½ steps (the same as a minor 3rd) and a diminished 7th consists of 4½ steps ( the same as a major 6th). Perfect intervals may be diminished or augmented but never become major or minor. Major intervals may be augmented but never become perfect. Minor intervals may be diminished but never become perfect.

Example 6

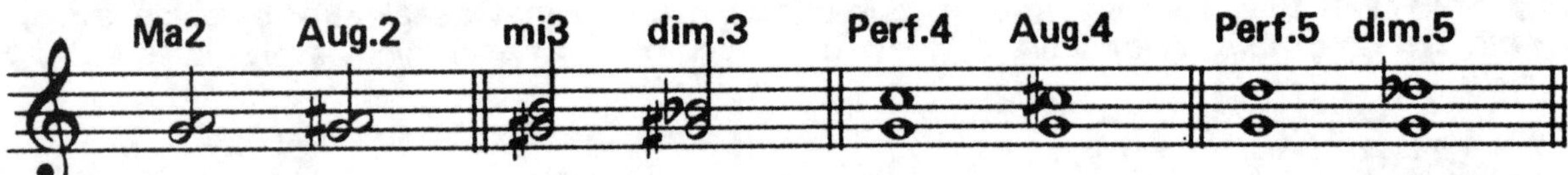


Each interval has a separate and unique expressive quality. Though the specific qualities of various intervals are hard to define exactly, composers have used intervals similarly for centuries. Certain musical effects seem to be universally true. For example, small melodic intervals tend to create a smooth, flowing effect

Example 7

Large melodic intervals tend to be stronger and more engaging, thus producing a more dramatic effect.

Example 8

Harmonic intervals can be generally arranged on a scale from consonance to dissonance. Thirds and 6ths tend to be more consonant, 2nds and 7ths tend to be more dissonant, while 4ths and 5ths are somewhat neutral depending on the context in which they are found. The following example shows one possible order on the scale.

Example 9

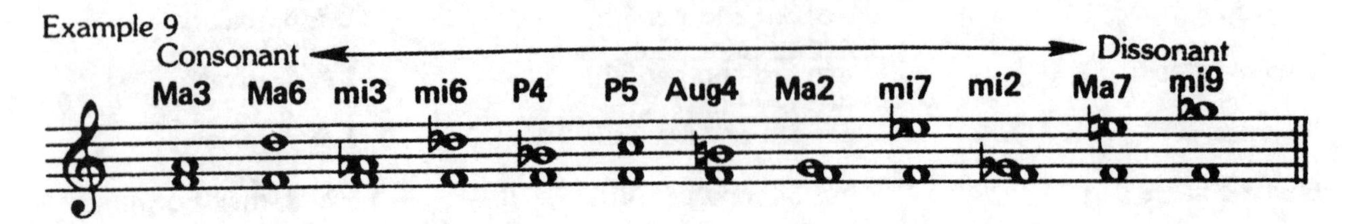

## Inversion of Intervals

Another aspect of intervals involves their inversion, or turning upside down. Understanding the laws of inversion can also be an aid in conceiving them. Basically, the following rules apply in the inversion of intervals: 1) the size of the interval and its inversion always totals 9. 2) a major interval inverts as a minor and vice versa. 3) an augmented interval inverts as a diminished and vice versa, and 4) perfect intervals remain perfect when inverted. Following are some typical examples of intervals and their inversions.

Example 10

mi3 Ma6 | Ma3 mi6 | Perf 4 Perf 5 | Aug 4 dim 5 | Aug 2 dim 7 | Ma 2 mi 7 | mi2 Ma 7

## Intervals Larger Than An Octave

Intervals larger than an octave are simply a combination of an octave and some smaller interval. Usually the quality of the interval will be consistent with its smaller counterpart. Following is an example of some common intervals which are larger than an octave.

Example 11

## STUDY QUESTIONS

1. Define the term interval in music.
2. What are the two general types of intervals?
3. Give three ways of conceiving intervals.
4. What are enharmonic intervals?
5. Which types of intervals can be augmented?
6. Which types of intervals can be diminished?
7. The size of an interval and its inversion always totals what number?
8. What does the quality of a major interval become when it is inverted?
9. What does the quality of an augmented interval become when it is inverted?
10. What intervals remain unchanged in quality when they are inverted?

## EXERCISES

Written:

1. Write the following intervals above and below the note F: mi2, ma2, mi3, ma3, Per4, Per5, mi6, ma6, mi7, ma7.
2. Write the following intervals above and below the note G: aug2, dim3, aug3, aug4, dim5, aug5, dim6, aug6, dim7.
3. Identify these intervals:

4. Identify these intervals:

Keyboard:

1. Play every interval up and down from each of the twelve chromatic pitches on the keyboard.
2. Play familiar melodies on the piano and analyze the intervals between each note.

Ear-training:

1. Sing all of the major, minor and perfect intervals up and down from a given pitch.
2. Make a list of song titles, each of which includes one of the following intervals in the first two or three notes: mi2 up mi2 down, ma2 up, ma2 down, mi3 up, mi3 down, ma3 up, ma3 down, P4 up, P4 down, Aug4 up, Aug4 down, P5 up P5 down, mi6 up, mi6 down, ma6 up, ma6 down, mi7 up, mi7 down, ma7 up, ma7 down.
   For example, P4 up: "Here Comes the Bride"; mi3 down: "Volga Boat Song".
3. Work with another person and practice identification of intervals upon hearing them.
4. Transcribe simple melodies from recordings. Test accuracy by playing along with the record.

## 2. BASIC CHORD CONSTRUCTION

### Triads

There are four basic types of triads (chords composed of three notes): major, minor, diminished and augmented. In popular music of the '70's, a variation of one of these occurs so frequently that it might almost be considered a fifth type. That is the sus4 chord. Example one shows all five types of triads.

Example 1

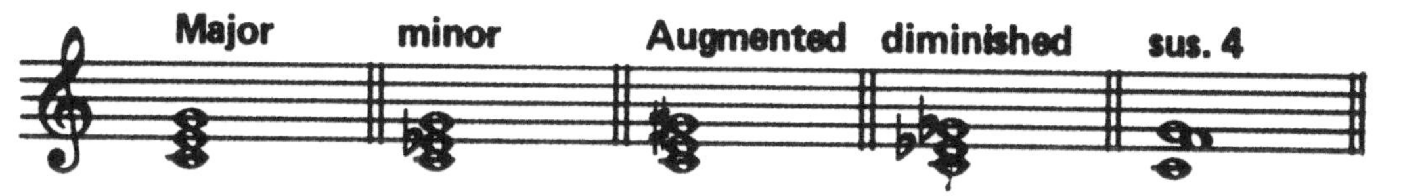


A major triad is composed of the 1st, 3rd and 5th notes of a major scale. Or it could be constructed by combining the intervals of a major 3rd and a minor 3rd.

Example 2

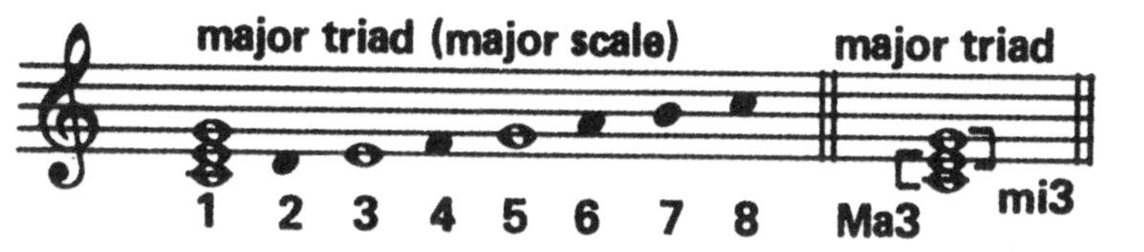


A minor triad is composed of the 1st, 3rd and 5th notes of a minor scale. Or it could be constructed by combining the intervals of a minor 3rd and a major 3rd.

Example 3

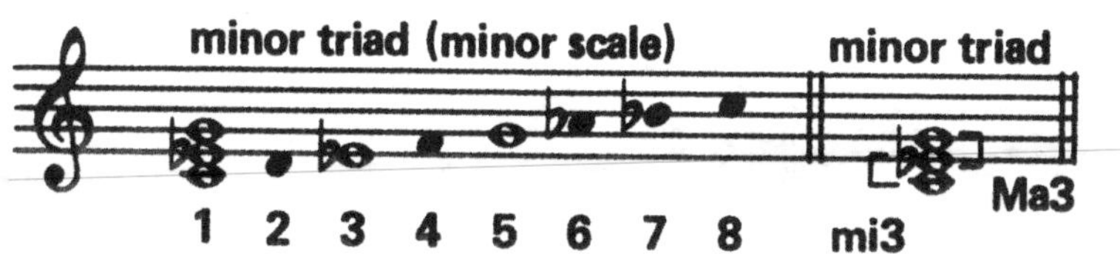


An augmented triad is a major triad with the 5th raised. A diminished triad is a minor triad with the 5th lowered.

Example 4

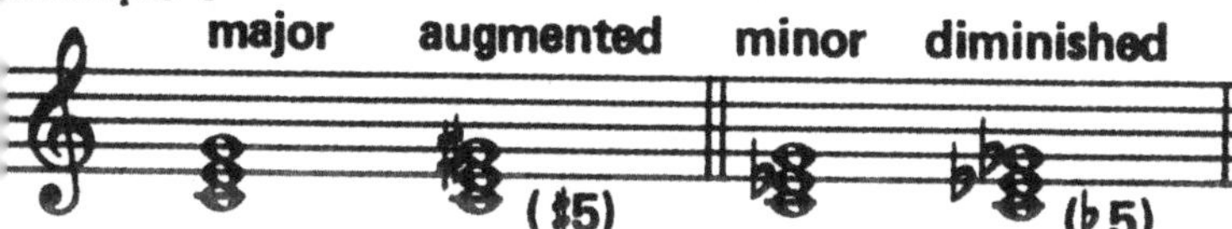


A sus4 chord is a major or minor triad in which the 4th scale step replaces the 3rd. In essence, the 4th is "suspended" from its resolution to the 3rd.

Example 5

### 6th Chords

A major 6th chord is a major triad with the addition of the 6th scale step from the major scale. A minor 6th chord uses the same 6th scale step as a major 6th chord.

Example 6

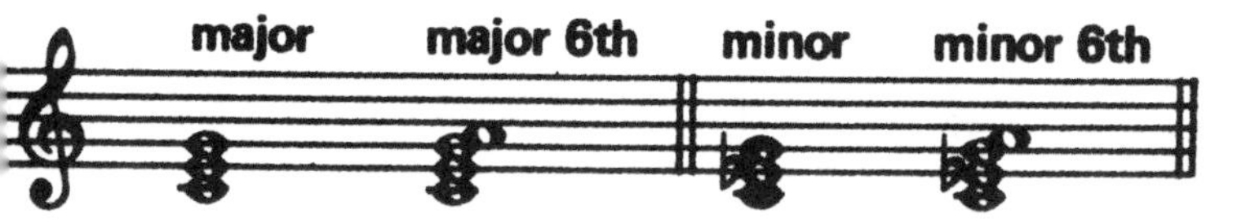

## 7th Chords

There are five types of 7th chords: major, dominant, minor, half-diminished and diminished. The following chart shows the interval structure and the tones of a major scale (either natural or lowered) that are used to construct each type of chord. The chords are shown in Ex. 7.

| Type of Seventh Chord | Interval Structure | Tones of the Major Scale |
|---|---|---|
| Major | ma3, mi3, ma3 | 1, 3, 5, 7 |
| dominant | ma3, mi3, mi3 | 1, 3, 5, ♭7 |
| minor | mi3, ma3, mi3 | 1, ♭3, 5, ♭7 |
| half-diminished | mi3, mi3, ma3 | 1, ♭3, ♭5, ♭7 |
| diminished | mi3, mi3, mi3 | 1, ♭3, ♭5, ♭♭7 |

Example 7

Normally, chords are built in 3rds, using every other note of the scale. Therefore, chord spellings for 7th chords involve every other letter of the musical alphabet. As a result, there are only seven different spellings for all 7th chords. Each of these spellings is adjusted with accidentals to conform to the correct key or chord type.

Example 8 shows several different chords based on the A, C, E, G chord spelling.

Example 8

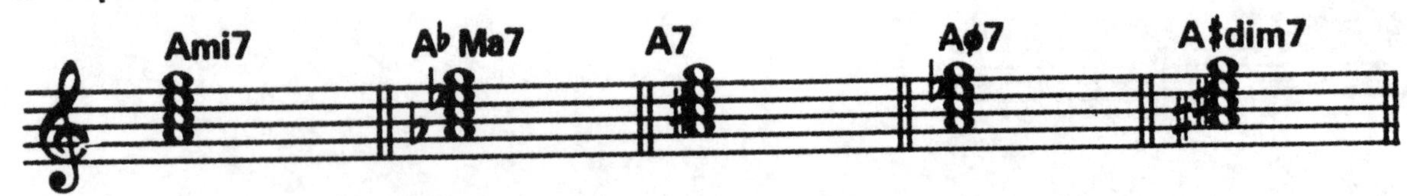


The seven possible spellings for 7th chords are:

A C E G, B D F A, C E G B, D F A C, E G B D, F A C E, G B D F.

Several alterations commonly occur in 7th chords. Major and dominant 7th chords may be augmented, that is, the 5th may be raised.

Example 9

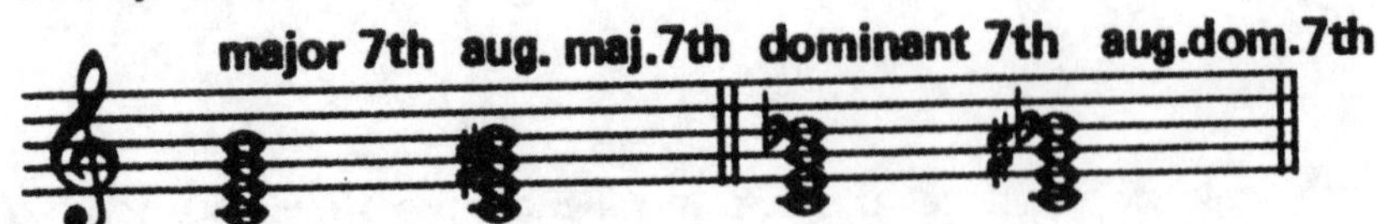


Minor 7ths sometimes have the 7th raised.

Example 10

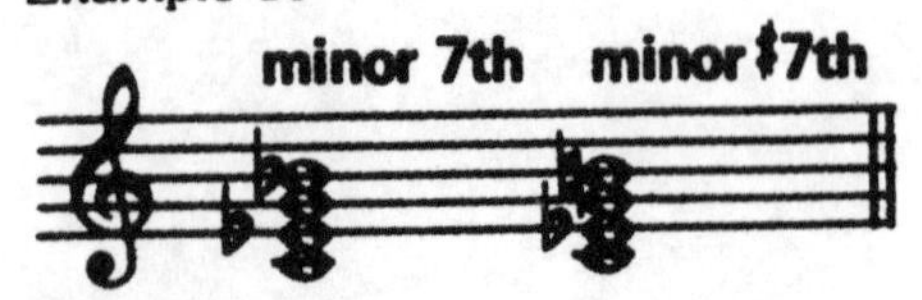


Major, minor or dominant 7ths may have the 4th suspended.

Example 11

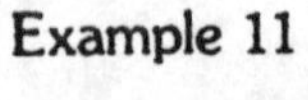

## Nomenclature

Nomenclature refers to the labeling and identification of the various chord types. Unfortunately, there is no one chord symbol for each type of chord that is universally agreed upon as the best. The following chart shows a recommended choice of chord symbol for each type of 7th chord plus several variations that are commonly used. The symbols are all in the key of C for comparison.

| Type of Seventh Chord | Recommended Symbol | Variations |
|---|---|---|
| C Major 7th | C Maj7 | CM7, Cma7, C△, C7 |
| C dominant 7th | C7 | C♭7 |
| C minor 7th | C min7 | Cm7, Cmi7, C-7 |
| C half-diminished 7th | C min7 ♭5 | Cø |
| C diminished 7th | C dim 7 | C°7, Cd7 |

A letter by itself indicates a major triad. A letter and a number other than 6 indicates a dominant chord. A plus (+) next to the key letter of a chord indicates that it is augmented.

Example 12

## STUDY QUESTIONS

1. What are the four basic types of triads?
2. Describe the construction of the four basic triads.
3. What is a sus4 chord?
4. A major or minor 6th chord is a triad with the addition of what scale step?
5. What are the five types of seventh chords?
6. Give the interval structure of each of the types of seventh chords.
7. What tones of the major scale are used to form each type of seventh chord?
8. Give the seven letter spellings for all seventh chords.
9. Give the recommended chord symbol for each of the five types of seventh chords.
10. What does a plus (+) next to the key-letter of a chord symbol indicate?

## EXERCISES

Written:

1. Write the following triads: D maj, F min, E aug, C♯ dim, E♭ maj, B min, A aug, B♭ dim, A♭ maj, F♯ min, D♭ aug, C dim.
2. Write the following sus4 chords: G sus4, A♭ sus4, F♯ sus4, D sus4, B♭ sus4.
3. Write the following 6th chords: C mi6, B♭6, A mi6, A♭6, F mi6, E6, E♭ mi6, D♭6, B mi6, G6.
4. Write the following 7th chords: C♯ maj7, D7, E♭ min7, E min7♭5, F dim7, G♭ maj7, F♯7, G min7, G♯min7♭5, A dim7, B♭ maj7, B7, C min7, C♯ min7♭5, D♯ dim7, D maj7, E7, F♯ min7, G dim7, B♭ min7♭5.

Keyboard:

1. In a given key, play the five types of triads: major, minor, augmented, diminished and sus4.
2. In a given key, play the five types of seventh chords: major, dominant, minor, half-diminished and diminished.
3. Play each of the types of triads or seventh chords in all keys.

Ear-training:

1. Sing each of the four basic triads from the root (1-3-5-3-1), 3rd (3-1-3-5-3), and the 5th (5-3-1-3-1).
2. Sing each of the five types of 7th chords from the root (1-3-5-7-5-3-1), the 3rd (3-1-3-5-7-5-3), the 5th (5-3-1-3-5-7-5), and the 7th (7-5-3-1-3-5-7).
3. Work with a friend and play triads and 7th chords for each other to practice identification.
4. Transcribe the harmony of simple compositions from recordings. Listen to the bass player to make sure what the root of the chord is and then sing the chord to test it. Choose pieces in which the harmonies last long enough to give you time to identify them.

## 3. MODES OF THE MAJOR SCALE

The major scale (also called Ionian mode) is well known to most young musicians since they are usually taught to play several of them early in their development. Though we usually play a major scale from its root to its root, there are several other modes (manners) in which it may be played. Each time it is played starting on a different note, the scale takes on a different quality. Accordingly, each one of these modes has a name to identify it. Following is a chart showing the order of the modes, their names and their location on the white notes of a piano. By visualizing the modes on the white notes it is very easy to see the location of the half steps since they occur between the notes E and F and B and C.

| Number of Mode | Name | Location on White Notes |
|---|---|---|
| 1st | Ionian | C to C |
| 2nd | Dorian | D to D |
| 3rd | Phrygian | E to E |
| 4th | Lydian | F to F |
| 5th | Mixolydian | G to G |
| 6th | Aeolian | A to A |
| 7th | Locrian | B to B |

Though it is easy to find the modes on the white notes of the piano, unfortunately they do not always occur in that key. Example 1 shows each of the modes built on the note C for comparison.

Example 1

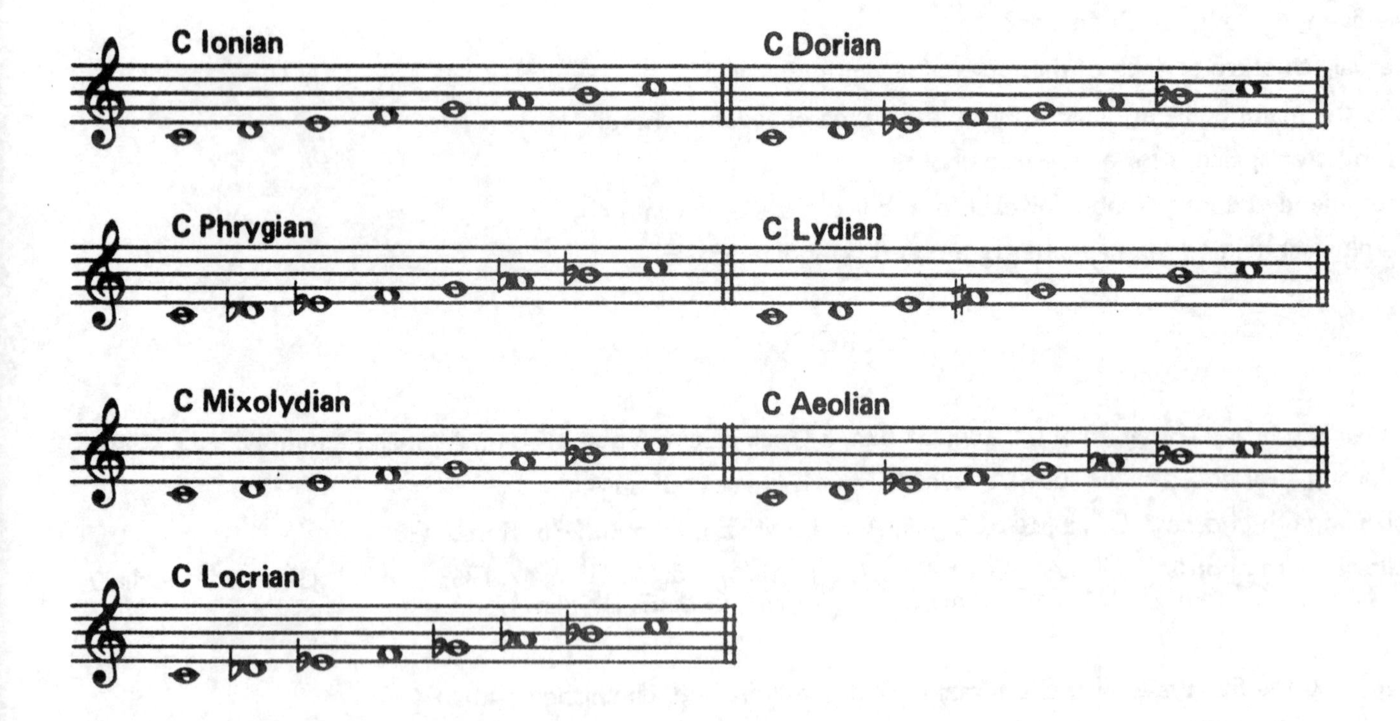


It should be apparent from the previous example that, to be able to construct any mode on a given note, a musician must have one or more ways of conceiving the structure of each mode. Actually, there are four excellent ways of conceiving the various modes which are as follows:

1. Find the location of the major key signature from which the mode is derived.
2. Locate the two half steps in the mode.
3. Alter a major or pure minor scale to create the mode.
4. Make adjustments to a major or minor key signature by adding or subtracting a sharp or flat.

The chart in Example 2 applies each of these ways of conceiving structure to each of the modes. Obviously, since Ionian (major) or Aeolian (pure minor) is the basis for conceiving other modes, not as many of these approaches are useful in constructing them.

Example 2

| Mode | Location of Major Key Signature | Location of Half-steps | Alterations to a Scale | Adjustments to a Major or Minor Key Signature |
|---|---|---|---|---|
| Ionian | Built on same note | Between 3 and 4 and 7 and 8 | None to a major scale | None to a major key signature |
| Dorian | A major 2nd below | Between 2 and 3 and 6 and 7 | 1) Pure minor with ♯6<br>2) Major with ♭3, ♭7 | Add a ♯ or subtract a ♭ from minor key |
| Phrygian | A major 3rd below | Between 1 and 2 and 5 and 6 | Pure minor with ♭2 | Add a ♭ or subtract a ♯ from minor key |
| Lydian | A perfect 4th below | Between 4 and 5 and 7 and 8 | Major with ♯4 | Add a ♯ or subtract a ♭ from major key |
| Mixolydian | A perfect 5th below or perfect 4th above | Between 3 and 4 and 6 and 7 | Major with ♭7 | Add a ♭ or subtract a ♯ from major key |
| Aeolian | A minor 3rd above | Between 2 and 3 and 5 and 6 | 1) None to a pure minor<br>2) Major with ♭3, ♭6, ♭7 | None to a minor key Signature |
| Locrian | A half step above | Between 1 and 2 and 4 and 5 | Pure minor with ♭2, ♭5 | Add 2♭'s or subtract 2♯'s from minor key* |

*Subtract a ♯ *and* add a ♭ to E pure minor to create E Locrian.

## Chord-Scale Relationships

Just as there is a mode beginning on each step of the major scale, there is a seventh chord built on each scale step which corresponds to the same mode. Example 3 shows the diatonic (scale derived) seventh chords of a C major scale.

Example 3

C Maj7 | D min7 | E min7 | F Maj7 | G7 | A min7 | B min7♭5

The following chart shows the relationship of each of the modes to its corresponding diatonic seventh chord.

| Scale Degree | Name of Mode | Quality of Mode | Quality of 7th Chord |
|---|---|---|---|
| I | Ionian | Major (♮4) | Major |
| II | Dorian | Minor (♯6) | Minor |
| III | Phrygian | Minor (♭2) | Minor |
| IV | Lydian | Major (♯4) | Major |
| V | Mixolydian | Major (♭7) | Dominant |
| VI | Aeolian | Minor (♮6) | Minor |
| VII | Locrian | Half-diminished | Half-diminished |

To use the modes effectively in composition or improvisation, it is essential to understand which tones (if any) are dissonant and need to resolve. The odd-numbered scale tones of each mode are chord tones of its corresponding 7th chord and are generally no problem. Dissonant tones which require special handling can be summarized as follows:

I. Ionian - The 4th scale step is dissonant and should resolve to the 3rd.

II. Dorian - Any scale degree may be stressed though some are more dissonant than others.

III. Phrygian - The 2nd and 6th scale steps are dissonant and should resolve downward by a half step.

IV. Lydian - Any scale degree may be stressed though some are more dissonant than others.

V. Mixolydian - The 4th scale step is dissonant and should resolve to the 3rd.

VI. Aeolian - The 6th scale step is dissonant and should resolve to the 5th.

VII. Locrian - The 2nd scale step is dissonant and should resolve to the 1st.

With four of the modes, we begin to see a comparison that shows the validity of two different traditions, the European classical tradition and the American jazz tradition. The classical tradition is instilled in us through our exposure to folk songs, hymns, classical music, camp songs etc. But, when involved in the jazz idiom, we often find the need for other resources that are peculiar to that tradition. Example 4 shows the relationship of two classical and two jazz scales to major and minor chords.

Example 4

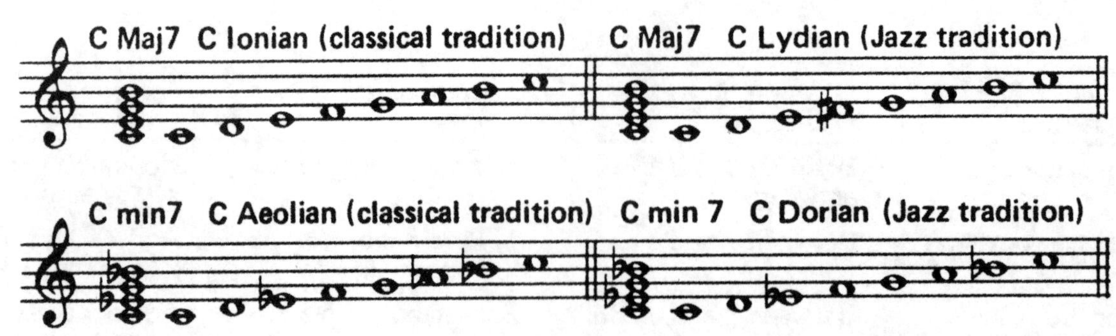


The important point to remember is that both traditions of music have validity and are of importance to the jazz musician. Even though some scales are not considered jazz scales as such, they very often serve certain musical situations as the most appropriate sounds to the flow of the composition. It would be very unwise to arbitrarily decide to always use Lydian with major chords or Dorian with minor chords. The relatively bland Ionian or Aeolian modes can sound extremely beautiful in many harmonic situations. The composer or improviser must experiment with all of the options available to him before deciding how to treat a piece of music. If he is really "in tune" with the flow of a piece, he will more than likely come up with an effective treatment of it!

## STUDY QUESTIONS

1. Name the seven modes of the major scale in order. Spell them correctly.
2. Explain the four ways of conceiving the modes.
3. Give the quality of each of the diatonic 7th chords of the major scale.
4. Discuss dissonant tones in the modes and their usual resolutions.
5. What are the two traditions that a jazz musician must be familiar with?

## EXERCISES

Written:

1. In a given key, write out all seven modes of the major scale. Do not use the key signature but rather locate the sharps or flats of the key in front of the appropriate notes.
2. Write all seven modes built on the same note. Use one of the four ways in example 2 to arrive at the proper set of notes.
3. Write the following modes: B♭Ionian, A Dorian, G Phrygian, F Lydian, E♭ Mixolydian, D Aeolian and C Locrian.
4. Write an eight measure melody in each mode. Be sure to stress scale tones that are unique to each mode and be careful of the handling of dissonant tones.

Keyboard:

1. Play a major scale in a given key. Then play all seven modes of that scale using the same fingering throughout.
2. Play all of the diatonic 7th chords of a given major scale. Put your thumb on the root of each chord regardless of whether it is a white note or a black note.

Ear-training:

1. Sing each of the modes from the root, up an octave and back again.
2. Sing each of the diatonic 7th chords of the major scale.
3. Working with another person, practice identification of the modes. Listen for the tones which are peculiar to each mode.
4. Listen for modes both in melodies and improvised solos on recordings. Transcribe and check by playing with the record.

## 4. BASIC SUBSTITUTION AND FUNCTION

As soon as a musician learns how to build chords he must then gain an understanding of how they are used in progressions. This involves learning how each type of chord may progress (function) and which chords substitute for each other to create slightly different effects.

Generally speaking, chords assume a function because of their location in a key. This also affects substitution possibilities since chords that function similarly may often substitute for each other. Example 1 shows the diatonic seventh chords in both major and minor. Notice that chords which are located on every other scale step have three tones in common. This shows the basis for common-tone chord substitution.

Example 1

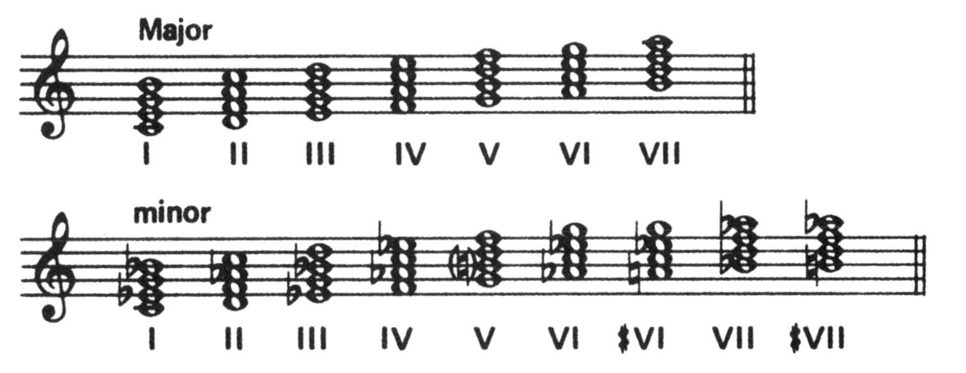


Notice that in a minor key the diatonic seventh chords are derived mainly from the pure minor scale except for the V, VI and VII chords which often involve the raised 6th or 7th scale step.

Since there are obvious differences in the diatonic seventh chords of either a major or minor key, the functions of each group will be discussed separately. Also, basic chord substitutes are summarized.

### Major Key Functions

| | |
|---|---|
| I Maj7 | Establishes the key center, doesn't need to progress, but may go anywhere. |
| II min7 | Substitute for IV Maj7; progresses to V (down a 5th) or to ♭II (down a half step). |
| III min7 | Substitute for I Maj7; progresses to VI (down a 5th) or to ♭III (down a half step). |
| IV Maj7 | Substitute for II min7; progresses to V; often serves as temporary key center for relief. |
| V dom7 | Progresses to I (down a 5th). |
| VI min7 | Substitute for I Maj7 or IV Maj7; progresses to II (down a 5th) or to ♭VI (down a half step); also is relative minor key center. |
| VII min7$^{\flat5}$ | Substitute for V7; progresses to I. |

### Minor Key Functions

| | |
|---|---|
| I min7 | Establishes the key center, doesn't need to progress, but may go anywhere. |
| II min7$^{\flat5}$ | Substitute for IV min7; progresses to V (down a 5th) or to ♭II (down a half step). |
| III Maj7 | Substitute for I min7; progresses to ♭VI (down a 5th) or to II (down a half step); also is the relative major key center. |
| IV min7 | Substitute for II min7$^{\flat5}$; progresses to V or to ♭VII (down a 5th); often serves as a temporary key center for relief. |
| V dom7 | Progresses to I (down a 5th). |
| VI Maj7 | Substitute for I min7 or IV min7; progresses to ♭II (down a 5th) or to V (down a half step). |
| ♮VI min7$^{\flat5}$ | Substitute for I min7; progresses to II (down a 5th) or to ♭VI (down a half step). |
| VII dom7 | Transitional chord between IV min7 and I; progresses to I or to ♭III (down a 5th). |
| ♮VII dim7 | Substitute for V7$^{\flat9}$; progresses to I. |

Some general conclusions may be drawn from the previous summaries of functions. They are as follow:

1) Major, minor and half-diminished 7th chords (min7$^{\flat5}$) have more then one normal function.
2) Dominant and diminished 7th chords commonly resolve to key center.
3) Many chords commonly progress either down a 5th or down a half step.

At this point something should be said about the nature of each family of chords.

*Major Family*

Since a major 7th chord is found built on the key center of a major scale, it can always assume a tonic (I) function regardless of its location in a key. In other words, it is relatively stable and doesn't need to progress to another chord.

Example 2

B♭7(V) | E♭Maj7(I) | D7(V) | G Maj7(I)

*Minor Family*

Since a minor 7th chord is found in five different locations in major or minor keys, it can assume more than one primary function. Its two most common functions are as either a tonic (I) chord in a minor key or a supertonic (II) chord in a major key. Therefore, a minor 7th can either be relatively stable or feel like it wants to progress down a 5th.

Example 3

G7(V) | C min7(I) | f♯min7(II) | B7(V)

*Dominant Family*

Since a dominant 7th chord is found built on the 5th scale step in either a major or minor key, it has a strong need to resolve down a 5th to the key center. A common exception is in a blues progression or simple one-chord rock tune where a dominant 7th often serves as the tonic (I) chord.

Example 4a

F7(V) | B♭Maj7(I) | A7(V) | Dmin7(I)

4b (Blues)

C7(I) | F7(IV) | C7(I)

*Half-diminished Chords*

Since a half-diminished 7th chord is found built on the 7th scale step of a major key, it may occur in a leading tone (VII) function and progress up a half step to the key center. However, a dominant 7th built on the 5th scale step is more often chosen as a chord to progress to tonic.

The most common function for a half-diminished chord is as a supertonic (II) chord in a minor key which progresses to the V chord. It is a fairly dissonant chord with a moderate need to progress, though not as strong as a dominant 7th.

Example 5

*Diminished Chords*

Since the only place a diminished 7th chord occurs is as a VII chord in a minor key, its function is that of a chord which may resolve up a half step to either a major or minor chord. The interesting thing about a diminished 7th chord is that, because of its symmetrical interval structure, it may be respelled as several different chords with several different resolutions. What tends to obscure the function is the fact that very often a diminished 7th chord may be spelled in one key but actually resolves as though it were spelled in a different key. This is done by the composer to create certain kinds of bass melodies in chord progressions. The important thing to remember is that a diminished 7th chord is a VII chord and will normally resolve either to a chord located a half step above any of its chord tones or to substitute for any of those chords. Example 6 shows several resolutions of the same diminished 7th chord sound with different spellings.

Example 6

B dim 7 | C min7 || A♭ dim7 | A♭ Maj7 || A♭dim7 | G min7

f dim7 | E♭ Maj7 || G♯dim7 | A Maj7 || D dim7 | B Maj7

## The II-V-I Progression

The II-V-I progression is one of the strongest and most common combinations of chords in jazz harmony. Many bebop tunes are composed using only chords which can be analyzed as either a II, V, or I chord in some major or minor key. Following is an explanation of the usual form of a II-V-I progression in both major and minor keys.

Major Key - II min7 to V7 to I Maj7
Minor Key - II min7♭5 to V7♭9 to I min7

There are hybrid combinations that depart from the normal form that may still be considered II-V-I. For example, II min7♭5 to V7♭9 to I Maj7 is a combination of the minor and major forms. Also, the II chord in either a major or minor key may sometimes be a dominant chord to produce an even stronger progression.

If the entire II-V-I unit is present in a chord progression, it is fairly easy to recognize. However, often only two of the three chords are present. Therefore, one must learn to recognize the smaller combinations such as II min7 to V7, II min7♭5 to V7♭9, V7 to I Maj7, and V7♭9 to I min7. Example 7 shows a progression involving chords which can all be analyzed as II, V, or I chords in major or minor keys.

Example 7

D7(V) G Maj7(I) f♯min7(II) B7(V) E Maj7(I) F7♭9(V) B♭min7(I)

Another common occurrence is a "chain", or series, or II-V progressions moving downward either in whole steps or half-steps.

Example 8

a) Emin7(II) A7(V) D min7(II) G7(V) C min7(II) F7(V)

b) E min7(II) A7(V) E♭ min7(II) A♭7(V) D min7(II) G7(V)

Some composers use a series of random V-I progressions to create sudden key changes.

Example 9

a) B Maj7(I) D7(V) G Maj7(I) B♭7(V) E♭ Maj7(I)

b) E min7(II) F7(V) B♭ Maj7(I) D♭ 7(V) G♭ Maj7(I) A7(V) D Maj7(I)

## Turn-around Progressions

An extension of the II-V-I progression is used to turn around from a I chord at the end of a phrase to start a new phrase on another I chord. It uses a VI chord to move away from I and move down a 5th to II. It has two basic forms in a major key and two forms in a minor key. Example 10 shows these common turn-arounds.

Example 10

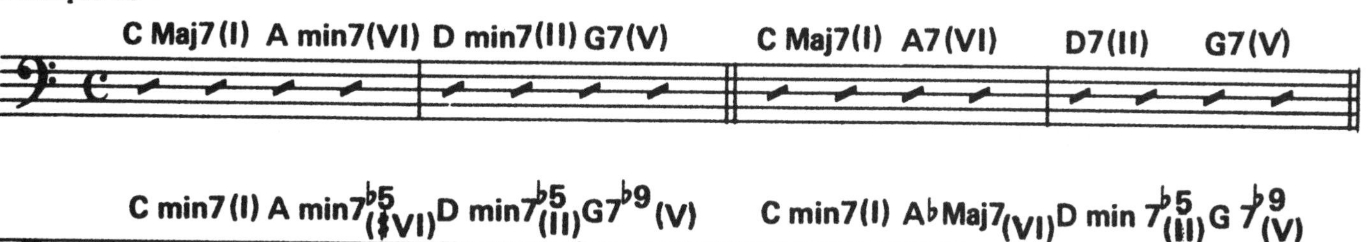

## Improving Progressions

Very often chord progressions can be improved by adding one or two chords in certain places. Chords are added in a strong functional relationship and are logical sounding as a result.

For example, when a tonic (I) chord of long duration occurs, it may be desirable to turn around rather than staying on one chord. Example 11 shows the original progression (a) and the improvement using a turn-around (b).

Example 11

a) C Maj.

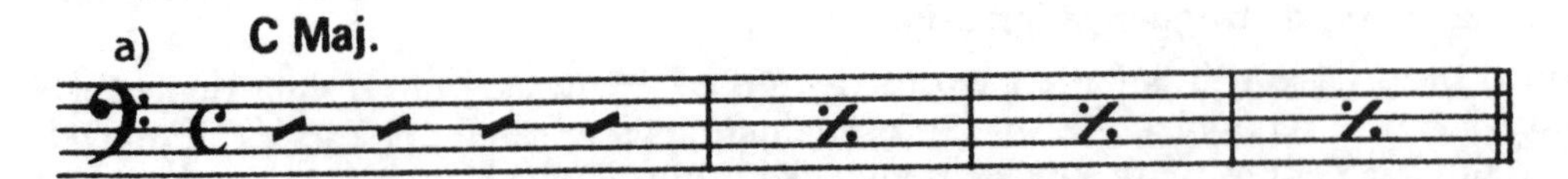

b) C Maj7 A min7 D min7 G7 C Maj7 A min7 D min7 G7

Very often a V chord of long duration occurs by itself in a progression to I. The improvement in this case is to add a II chord splitting the duration of the V between the two chords.

Example 12

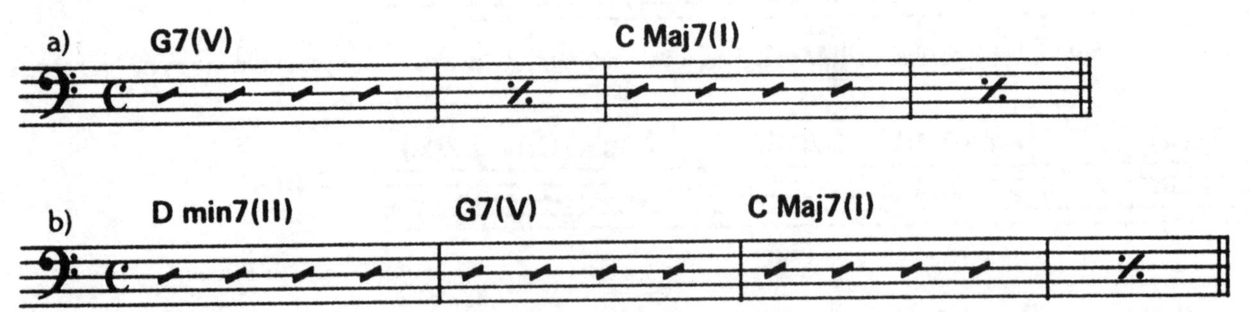


In a minor key when a I chord of long duration occurs, sometimes it can be treated as though it is a II chord and add the dominant chord a 5th below. This adds harmonic motion without really changing the sound drastically.

Example 13

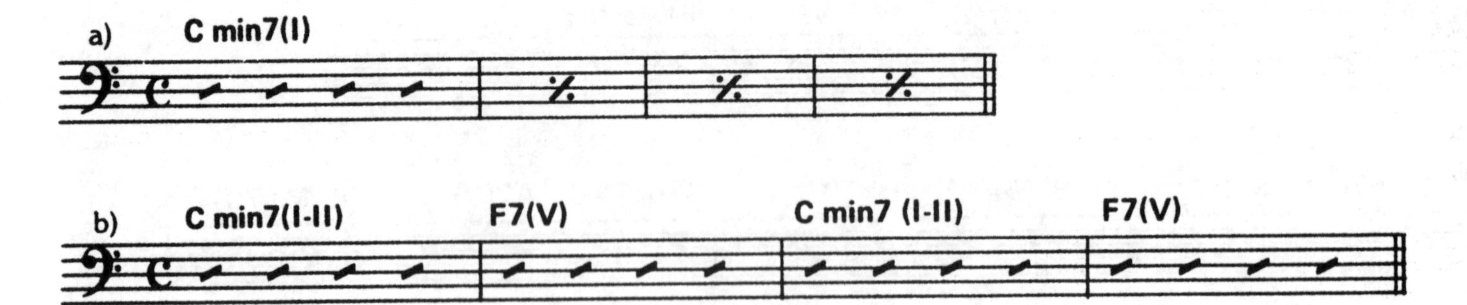


## STUDY QUESTIONS

1. Describe the quality of each diatonic seventh chord in a major key. Also give the substitute(s) and typical progression(s) of each.
2. Describe the quality of each diatonic seventh chord in a minor key. Also give the substitute(s) and typical progression(s) of each.
3. What is the general relationship of chords which substitute for each other?
4. What general conclusions may be drawn concerning chord function?
5. Discuss the nature of each family of chords with regard to function.
6. Give the usual format of a II-V-I progression in both a major key and a minor key.
7. What is a simple turn-around progression?

## EXERCISES

Written:

1. On staff paper, write out the diatonic seventh chords of a given major key including the proper Roman Numeral identification of each (I Maj7, II min7, etc.)
2. On staff paper, write out the diatonic seventh chords of a given minor key including the proper Roman Numeral identification of each (I min7, II min7♭5, etc.).
3. Analyze the following progressions by placing a Roman Numeral above each chord to show its location in either a major or minor key:

   a) G Maj7  E mi7  A mi7  D7  B mi7  C Maj7  A mi7  D7  E mi7  C Maj7  D7  B mi7  E mi7  A mi7  F♯ mi7♭5
   G Maj7  C Maj7  A mi7  D7  G Maj7

   b) D mi7  E mi7♭5  A7♭9  D mi7  B mi7♭5  E mi7♭5  A7  F Maj7  B♭ Maj7  G mi7  A7  D mi7  B♭ Maj7
   E mi7♭5  A7  G mi7  E mi7♭5  A7♭9  C♯ dim7  D mi7

4. Analyze the following progressions by bracketing key areas and placing a Roman Numeral above each chord to show its location in the particular key:

   a) E♭ Maj7  C mi7  F mi7  B♭7  B mi7  E7  A Maj7  B♭ mi7  E♭7  A mi7♭5  F♯ dim7  G mi7  A7  D Maj7
   C mi7  F7  B♭ Maj7  F♯ mi7♭5  B7♭9  E mi7

   b) G mi7  C7  F Maj7  F♯ mi7  B7  F mi7  B♭7  E mi7  A7  D Maj7  C mi7♭5  F7♭9  B♭ mi7  A mi7  D7
   G Maj7  G♯ dim7  A mi7  A♭7  D♭ Maj7

Keyboard:

1. Play all of the diatonic seventh chords of a given major key in root position.
2. Play all of the diatonic seventh chords of a given minor key in root position.
3. Transpose the II-V-I progressions shown in Example 14 to every major or minor key and learn to play by memory.

Example 14

IImin7  V7  IMaj7  IImin7♭5  V7♭9  I min7

4. Transpose the turn-around progressions shown in Example 15 to every major or minor key and learn to play by memory.

Example 15

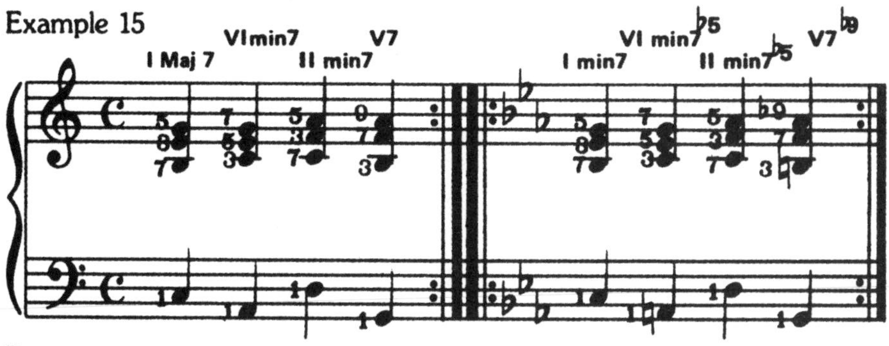


Ear-training:

1. Sing each of the diatonic 7th chords of the minor scale.
2. Sing a diminished 7th chord from the root (1-3-5-7-5-3-1), the 3rd (3-1-3-5-7-5-3), the 5th (5-3-1-3-5-7-5) and the 7th (7-5-3-1-3-5-7).
3. Working with another person, practice identification of the quality and location of diatonic 7th chords in both major and minor keys.
4. Transcribe the harmonies of compositions from recordings. Listen for the occurrence of common functions such as II-V, V-I, and II-V-I in major and minor keys.

## 5. THIRTEENTH CHORDS

Seventh chords are built by using the odd-numbered scale tones (1, 3, 5 and 7). If one continues to count on up through the scale, still using the odd-numbered scale tones, the 9th, 11th and 13th of a chord may be found. The 15th scale step is a repetition of the root (1st scale step) so, normally, chords larger than 13th chords cannot be constructed.

The three types of thirteenth chords with which jazz musicians are usually involved are major, dominant and minor. Half-diminished chords larger than 9th chords are rare and diminished chords cannot be larger than 7th chords because of their symmetrical structure. Example 1 shows the three types of 13th chords built on the root C.

Example 1

In Example 1, notice that the 11th scale degree has been raised in the major and dominant 13th chords. This is generally understood to be necessary to avoid a clash of the natural 11th and the 3rd of the chord. The only reason that the 11th would not be raised in those two types of 13th chords is if the 3rd was omitted from them. In fact, if a chord symbol specifies a natural 11th in a dominant chord, this generally implies that the 3rd is omitted.

Example 2

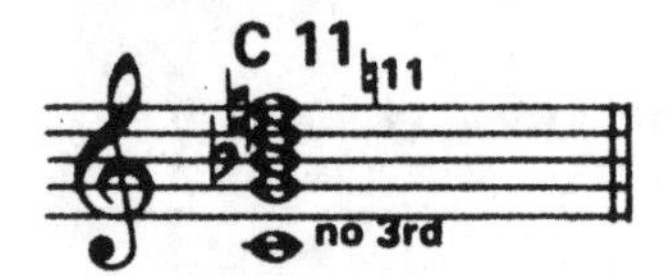


The minor 13th chord requires no alteration of the 11th since the 3rd is lowered and no clash occurs between those two chord tones.

Thirteenth chords are generally considered to be complex chords, both in their sound and in their construction. However, a closer look reveals that 13th chords can be constructed by combining the appropriate type of 7th chord with either a major or minor triad. Example 3 shows the three types of 13th chords again. However, this time each is described as a combination of two separate chords.

Example 3

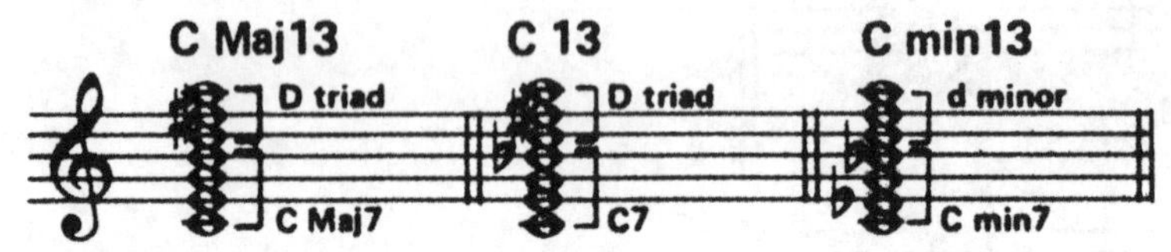


This leads to the development of formulas for building 13th chords easily. To construct a 13th chord, one begins with the appropriate type of 7th chord (major for major 13th, dominant for dominant 13th, minor for minor 13th). Then a triad, whose root is located a whole step above that of the seventh chord, is added to complete the chord. For a major or dominant 13th chord, the triad is major; for a minor 13th chord, the triad is minor.

Following is a summary of the formulas for 13th chords:

Major 13th chord = Major triad / Major 7th chord

Dominant 13th chord = Major triad / Dominant 7th chord

Minor 13th chord = Minor triad / Minor 7th chord

Specifically, the equations for the 13th chords in Example 3 would be as follows:

C Maj 13 = D/C Maj 7
C 13 = D/C7
C min 13 = D min/C min 7

Once it is understood how to construct a 13th chord, the musician must decide whether he wants to select only certain tones for a particular musical effect. For example, in voicing a 13th chord, a pianist may choose to play only the 3rd, 7th, 9th and 13th of the chord and omit the root, 5th and 11th chord tones. However, there are certain considerations of which a player or writer should be aware in making these choices. The following is a summary of the status of the various chord members of a 13th chord:

| | | |
|---|---|---|
| Root | - | May be included for strength or may be omitted. |
| 3rd | - | Important color tone, normally present except in sus4 chord. |
| 5th | - | May be omitted unless it is altered. |
| 7th | - | Important color tone, normally present except in $\frac{9}{6}$ chord. |
| 9th | - | Optional color tone unless specifically called for. |
| 11th | - | Optional color tone (same as 9th). |
| 13th | - | Optional color tone (same as 9th). |

It should be apparent that the 9th, 11th and 13th chord tones are all optional and may be included or omitted in any combination. For example, a chord may have an 11th but no 9th or 13th or it may have a 13th but not include the 9th or 11th. This is purely a matter of personal taste unless the composer specifies a particular extension of the harmony. The 3rd and 7th continue to be the most important color tones which define the quality of the chord and the upper extensions are only an elaboration of the sound.

In using 13th chords, it is important to remember that the size of a chord has no effect on the way that it functions. For example, a dominant 13th functions the same way that a dominant 7th chord built on the same root would. A minor 11th chord can occur in the same harmonic situation that a minor 7th could. Chords are grouped in related families (major, minor, etc.) because they sound basically the same and function the same. Increasing the size of a chord tends to add fullness and often makes the harmony more dissonant. However, the basic quality of the chord is still heard (felt) as being the same, so the overall musical effect is not drastically changed. In choosing the size of chord to be used (triad, 7th, 9th, 11th or 13th), the musician must always try to determine what is the most appropriate sound for the style of music with which he is involved. In a pop-rock style, the triad may be the best choice whereas, in a complex jazz idiom, 11th and 13th chords may be the most appropriate. Ultimately, the only way to develop those instincts is by playing, writing and listening to a great deal of music.

## STUDY QUESTIONS

1. How are 13th chords normally constructed using scale tones?
2. What are the three types of 13th chords normally used?
3. Why is the 11th scale step usually raised in major and dominant 13th chords? Why does it not have to be raised in a minor 13th chord?
4. What are the formulas for constructing 13th chords by combining two smaller chords?
5. What is the status of each of the chord members of a 13th chord as far as its inclusion or omission?
6. Does the size of a chord affect the way it functions in harmony?
7. What are chord families?

## EXERCISES

Written:

1. On staff paper, write out the following 13th chords in root position:
   D Maj13, A♭ 13, F♯ mi13, G Maj13, E 13, B♭ mi13, E♭ Maj13, A♭ mi13, D♭ 13, B Maj13.
2. Identify the following 13th chords:

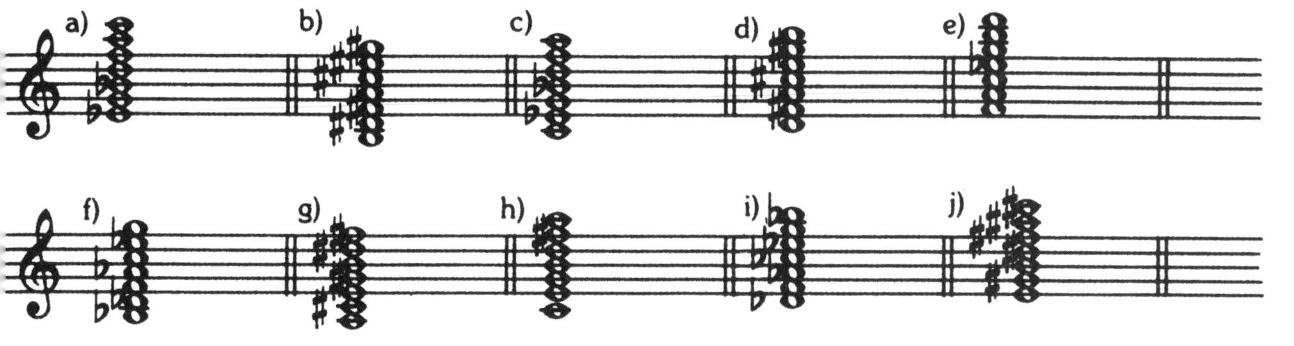


3. Convert the following chord symbols to polychord symbols which represent the same chords:
   D 13, A Maj13, G mi13, B♭ 13, D♭ Maj13, E mi13, F 13, F Maj13, C♯ mi13, A 13.

Keyboard:

1. Play 13th chords in all keys. Play the root, 3rd, 5th and 7th (basic 7th chord) in the left hand and play the 9th, 11th and 13th (major or minor triad) in the right hand. This will help you to visualize the two separate parts of each polychord.
2. Try playing voicings which include only certain tones of 13th chords such as 3-7-9-11 or 7-3-6(13)-9. Build these voicings from the first number upwards on major, minor and dominant 13ths.

Ear-Training:

1. Sing major, minor and dominant 13th chords upwards from the root and back down again (1-3-5-7-9-11-13-11-9-7-5-3-1).
2. Working with a friend, learn to identify major, minor and dominant 13th chords in root position when you hear them.
3. Listen for the presence of 9ths, 11ths and 13ths in the voicings which piano, quitar and vibes players use on recordings. Transcribe your favorites and analyze them for future use.

## 6. MODES OF THE HARMONIC MINOR SCALE

The harmonic minor scale is one of three traditional forms of minor scale. The *pure minor* scale occurs as the 6th mode (aeolian) of the major scale. The *ascending melodic minor* will be studied in Chapter 8. This chapter will deal with the third form, the *harmonic minor* scale.

The harmonic minor scale is constructed by raising the 7th scale degree of a pure minor scale one half-step. This creates a scale with a unique quality since it includes an interval of an augmented 2nd between the 6th and 7th scale steps. In traditional music, the augmented 2nd was considered an awkward melodic interval and, accordingly, this form of the minor scale was not as commonly used as were the other two. However, the harmonic minor scale generates a series of modes that are very useful in the jazz idiom as will soon be discovered.

By its nature (an alteration of pure minor), the harmonic minor scale cannot be conveniently conceived using conventional key signatures. Also, with the exception of the first one, the modes of this scale normally do not have universal names such as dorian or lydian. Consequently, they are usually identified by their numerical position in the scale (2nd mode, 5th mode, etc.). In Example 1, the modes of a C harmonic minor scale are written out in order.

Example 1

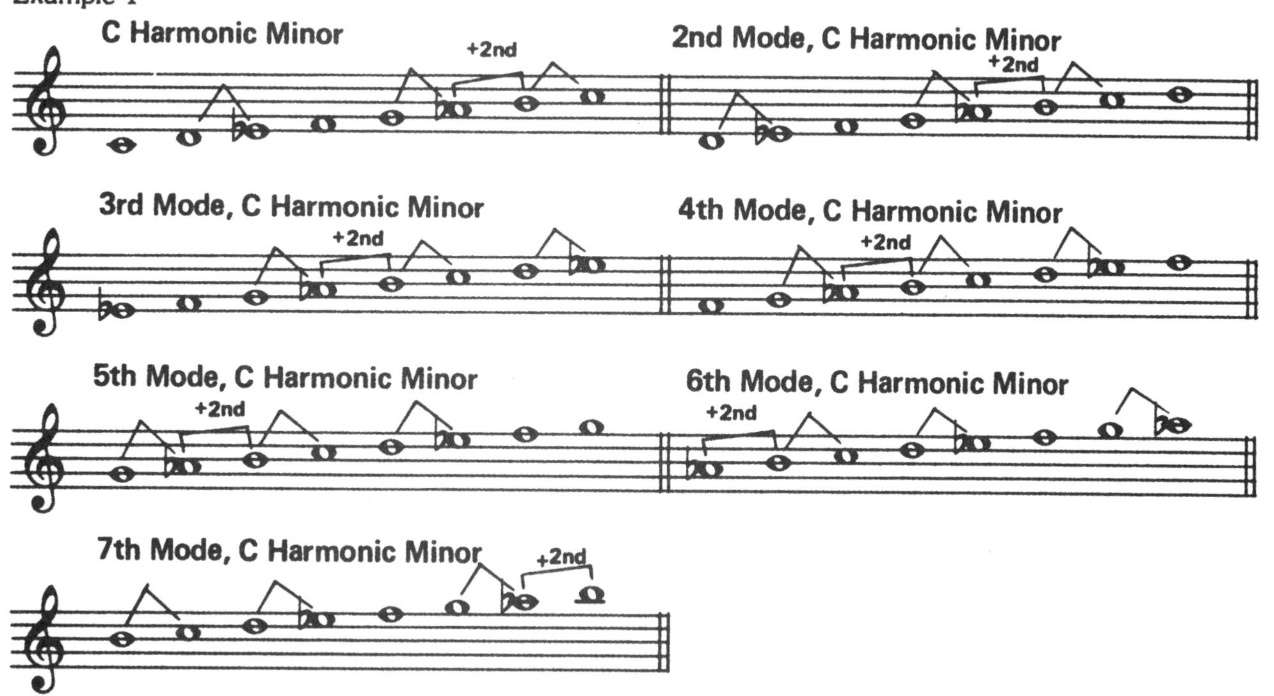


Notice in Example 1 that the location of the three half-steps and the augmented 2nd have been indicated. This can be a definite aid in learning their construction. However, it will probably be easiest to locate the "parent" key when constructing a particular mode. For example, if the 5th mode is desired, simply think of the harmonic minor key located a perfect 5th below. Example 2 shows all seven modes of the harmonic minor scale built on the note C with the "parent" key indicated in parentheses.

Example 2

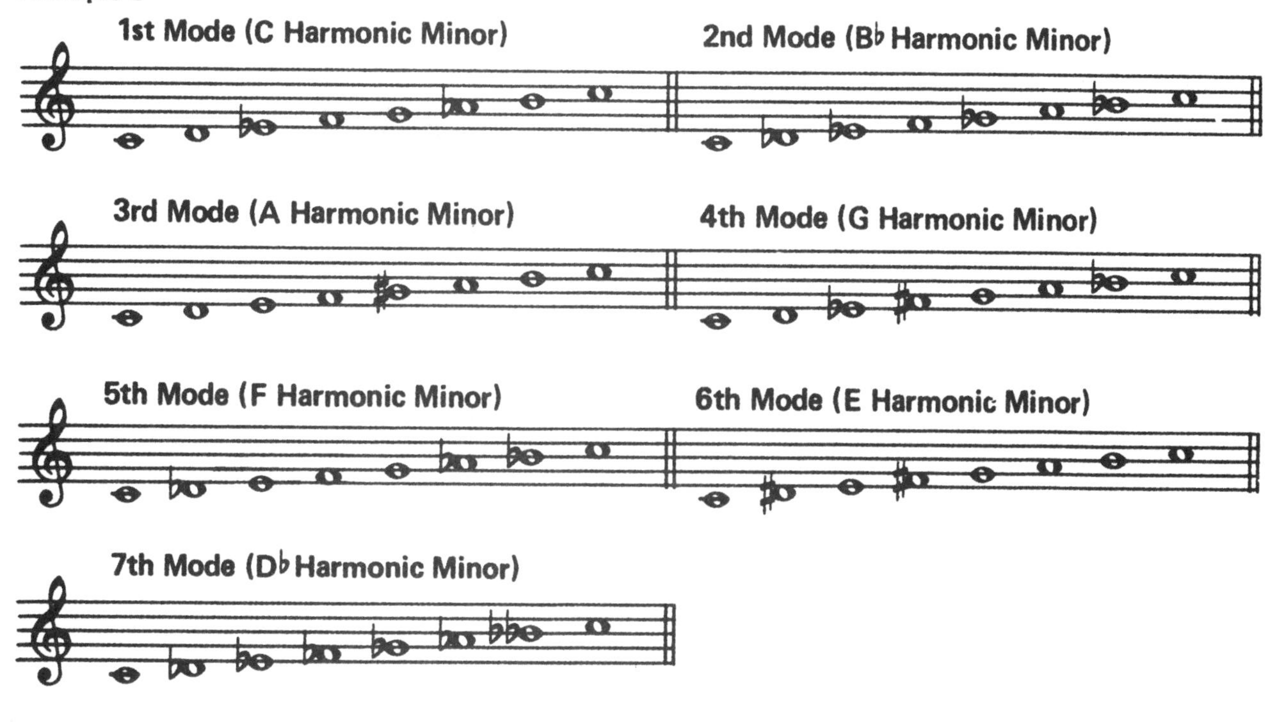

## Chord-Scale Relationships

In studying the modes of the major scale, it was found that each mode has a corresponding diatonic seventh chord. The diatonic seventh chords of the harmonic minor scale are somewhat more unusual because of the structure of the scale. Example 3 shows the diatonic (scale derived) seventh chords of a C harmonic minor scale.

Example 3

The following chart shows the relationship of each of the modes to its corresponding diatonic seventh chord:

| Scale Degree | Identification of Mode | Quality of Mode | Quality of 7th chord |
|---|---|---|---|
| I | Harmonic Minor | Minor (♯7) | Minor, ♯7 |
| II | 2nd Mode of Harm. Min. | Half-diminished | Half-diminished |
| III | 3rd Mode of H. M. | Major (♯5) | Major, ♯5 |
| IV | 4th Mode of H.M. | Minor (♯4) | Minor |
| V | 5th Mode of H. M. | Major (♭2, ♭6, ♭7) | Dominant, ♭9, ♭13 |
| VI | 6th Mode of H. M. | Major (♯2, ♯4) | Major, ♯11 |
| VII | 7th Mode of H. M. | Diminished | Diminished |

From the previous chart, it can be seen that this group of modes can be used with some colorful harmonies not served by modes of the major scale. However, as before, it is essential to understand the nature of each mode to use it effectively in composition or improvisation. Again, the odd-numbered scale tones of each mode are chord tones of its corresponding 7th chord and are generally not a problem. Dissonant tones which require special handling can be summarized as follows:

| | | |
|---|---|---|
| I | Harmonic Minor | The 6th scale step is dissonant and should resolve to the 5th. |
| II | 2nd Mode | The 2nd and 6th scale steps are dissonant and should resolve to the 1st and 7th respectively. |
| III | 3rd Mode | The 4th and 6th scale steps are dissonant and should resolve to the 3rd and 5th respectively. |
| IV | 4th Mode | The 4th scale step is dissonant and should resolve to the 5th. |
| V | 5th Mode | Used with a Dom 7, ♭9, ♭13, the 4th and 5th scale steps are dissonant and should resolve to the 3rd and 6th respectively. |
| VI | 6th Mode | The 2nd scale step is dissonant and should resolve to the 3rd. |
| VII | 7th Mode | The 2nd and 4th scale steps are dissonant and should resolve to the 1st and 3rd respectively. |

As in Chapter 3, we discover once more how useful a rather traditional scale form is to the jazz musician. An analysis of improvised solos by players whose roots are in the bebop era will reveal extensive use of the harmonic minor scale and some of its modes. In music of the seventies, all modes of this scale were commonly used by some musicians. Remember, the manner in which scale materials are used is responsible for the idiom or style created, not the scales themselves!

## STUDY QUESTIONS

1. What are the three traditional forms of minor scales?
2. How are the modes of the harmonic minor scale usually identified?
3. What is the structure of a harmonic minor scale?
4. Can a harmonic minor scale be represented by a key signature?
5. What is meant by the "parent" key of a mode?
6. What is probably the easiest way to conceive the various modes of a harmonic minor scale?
7. Give the quality of each of the diatonic 7th chords of a harmonic minor scale.
8. Discuss dissonant tones in the modes and their usual resolutions.
9. Are some scales more contemporary or traditional than others?

## EXERCISES

Written:

1. In a given key, write out all seven modes of the harmonic minor scale. Do not use a key signature but rather locate the sharps or flats of the scale in front of the appropriate notes.
2. Write all seven modes of the harmonic minor built on the same note. Write the "parent" key above each mode.
3. Write the following modes: 3rd mode of A harmonic; 5th mode of G harmonic; 2nd mode of D harmonic; 7th mode of E♭ harmonic; 4th mode of F♯ harmonic; 6th mode of F harmonic; 2nd mode of B harmonic; 5th mode of E harmonic; 3rd mode of B♭ harmonic; and 7th mode of A♭ harmonic.
4. Write an eight measure melody in each mode. Be sure to stress scale tones that are unique to each mode and be careful of the handling of dissonant tones.

Keyboard:

1. Play a harmonic scale in a given key. Then play all seven modes of it using the same fingering throughout.
2. Play all of the diatonic 7th chords of a given harmonic minor scale. Put your thumb on the root of each chord regardless of whether it is a white note or a black note.

Ear-Training:

1. Sing each of the modes of the harmonic minor from the root, up an octave and back again.
2. Sing each of the diatonic 7th chords of the harmonic minor scale.
3. Working with another person, practice identification of the modes.
4. Listen for the use of harmonic minor in improvised solos on recordings. Transcribe and check by playing with the record.

## 7. VOICING AND CONNECTING CHORDS

So far, the structure of 7th chords and 13th chords has been studied. The primary concern has been to ascertain the correct chord tones for the various types of chords. But, once this has been done, the musician must decide which chord tones to include or omit and how to make the harmony flow smoothly. Voicing chords is simply the process of selecting certain chord tones and arranging them in a particular order from top to bottom. An understanding of principles of voicing and connecting chords is important not only to writers and keyboard players but to improvisers as well. All musicians must have a good understanding of the structural framework of music.

This chapter will deal primarily with four three-note voicings which have shown themselves to be extremely flexible and useful in the majority of harmonic situations. By limiting the number of choices to only four voicings, it will simplify learning the basic principle of chord connection. Also, it will be seen that these voicings concentrate on the most important color tones and result in a strong sounding of the harmony with a minimum of tones. Example 1 shows the four voicings with which you will be concerned.

Example 1

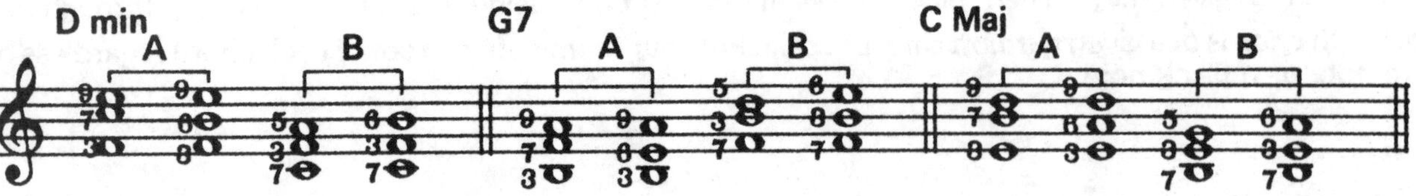

D min A B G7 A B C Maj A B

Notice that the Category A voicings in Example 1 are built on the 3rd of the chord (lowest tone) and the Category B voicings are built on the 7th. Voicings other than these two types may certainly be used but are really not necessary for some time. Also, as soon as one learns to use these simple "shells" of the harmony correctly, it is a simple matter to fill in any of the three-note voicings with a fourth chord tone to fill it out more or to account for some other needed chord member. However, for the present, only these four three-note voicings will be used exclusively!

Generally speaking, any of the four voicings in Example 1 can be used with major, minor or dominant family chords. However, there are a few considerations and the following chart is a summary of those:

| | MAJOR FAMILY | DOMINANT FAMILY | MINOR FAMILY |
|---|---|---|---|
| 9<br>7<br>3 | Good | Good | Good |
| 9<br>6<br>3 | Good | Avoid! | Good except for II Chord |
| 6<br>3<br>7 | Good | Good | Good except for II chord. |
| 5<br>3<br>7 | Good | Good | Good |

For the present, only one of the voicings can be used with a half-diminished chord: 7, 3, 5. This is because a half-diminished chord is really the same thing as a minor 7th chord with a lowered 5th. Therefore, the 5th becomes an important distinguishing color tone which should be present to acheive the proper chord quality. Later, the 5th may be added into a 3, 7, 9 voicing to complete the sound.

Since diminished 7th chords are symmetrical chords which seem to have no one root, any three of the four chord tones generally may be chosen. The context in which it is found will have some effect on this choice. However, since diminished chords occur less frequently, we will be concerned primarily with major, dominant, minor and half-diminished chords ar first.

Naturally, the first priority if to learn to spell the four voicings as they relate to various chord families in any key. This can be practiced in several ways:

1) Spell all four voicings as they relate to major, dominant and minor chords in one given key.
2) Spell one type of-voicing as it relates to major, dominant *or* minor chords in every key.
3) Combine methods 1 and 2. For example: spell a 3, 7, 9 voicing as it relates to a major chord in every key, then a dominant chord in every key and finally a minor chord.

## GUIDELINES FOR THE CONNECTION OF VOICINGS

As soon as some fluency in spelling voicings is gained, the next step is to learn how to connect one voicing to another. Example 2 shows a number of short chord progressions with typical uses of the four voicings presented in this chapter.

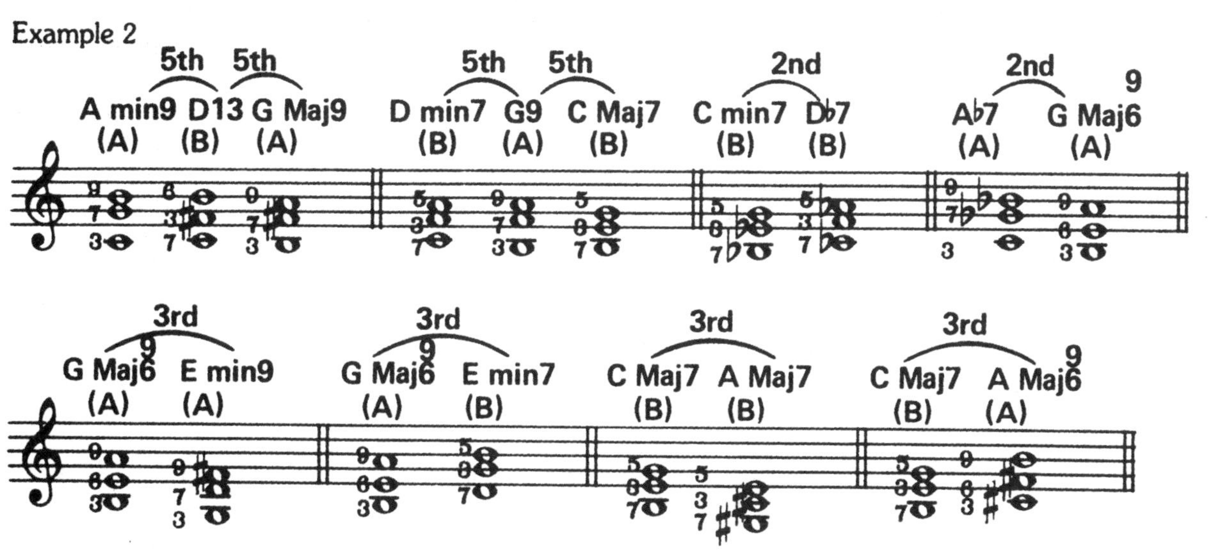


In Example 2, notice that there is as little vertical motion as possible in moving from one voicing to another. A minimum amount of motion in connecting chord voicings has several important advantages:

1) It eliminates unnecessary motion for a keyboard player.
2) In arrangements for horns, it helps avoid awkward angular melodic motion in inner parts.
3) It creates the smoothest possible flow in the music.

Though there are no rules as such, it will be helpful to follow certain steps in selecting voicings for a series of chords in a progression. They are as follows:

1) *Analyze the type of progression.*

What is the actual distance between the roots of the chords? All progressions can be summarized as either a progression of a 5th (inversion of a 4th), progression of a 2nd (inversion of a 7th), or progression of a 3rd (inversion of a 6th). Always reduce the interval to its simplest terms, i.e., a minor 3rd rather than an augmented 2nd, or a major 3rd rather than a diminished 4th.

2) *Choose the proper category of voicing (A or B).*

Keep in mind the following factors:
a) Progression of a 5th (4th) - Change category (A to B, B to A)
b) Progression of a 2nd (7th) - Keep the same category.
C) Progression of a 3rd (6th) - Either change category or keep the same category. It may be desirable to move to a higher register or to a particular voicing.

3) *Write the specific voicing.*

Keep in mind the function, register, and a smooth flow from voicing to voicing.

Generally speaking, it would be a good idea to keep the voicing as close to middle C on the piano as possible. This will insure that the voicing is neither muddy nor thin and has good clarity and fullness. Other notes may be added to fill out these shells later.

Now go back and look at Example 2 again and observe how the guidelines have been followed. Notice that the distance between the roots is indicated above each pair of chords. Also, notice that the proper category of voicing has been chosen according to the type of progression. Finally, you should realize that none of the minor II chords use a voicing with a 6th in it and that all of the dominant 7th chords include a 7th in the voicing.

## STUDY QUESTIONS

1. What is meant by the term "voicing chords"?
2. What are the four voicings introduced in this chapter?
3. What are Category A and Category B voicings?
4. What considerations affect the use of certain voicings?
5. For the present, what voicing is the only choice for a half-diminished chord?
6. Why does one try to use as little vertical motion as possible in moving from one voicing to another?
7. What are the three guidelines for the connection of voicings?
8. What are the three types of root progressions and how do they affect the choice of category of a voicing?

# EXERCISES

Written:

1. Spell 3, 7, 9 voicings on the following: D Maj7, G min7, E♭7, G♭ Maj7, F min7, B Maj7, A7, E7, B♭ min7, and C♯ min7.
2. Spell 3, 6, 9 voicings on the following: D♭ Maj, C min, B min, G Maj, F Maj, E♭ min, F♯ min, A♭ Maj, E Maj, and D min.
3. Spell 7, 3, 6 voicings on the following: B♭7, A Maj7, F min7, E♭ Maj7, D7, A♭ min7, E Maj 7, G7, C min7, and B♭ Maj7.
4. Spell 7, 3, 5 voicings on the following half-diminished chords: C, C♯, D, E , F, F♯, G, G♯, A and B.
5. Write voicings for the following chord progressions (Begin with a 7, 3, 5 voicing in each exercise):
   a) E♭ Maj7 D min7$^{\flat 5}$ G7$^{\flat 9}$ C min7 B♭ min7 E♭7 F♯ min7 B7$^{\sharp 5}$ E Maj7 F7$^{\sharp 9}$ B♭ Maj7$^{\flat 5}$
   b) C min7 D min7 E♭ min7 A♭7$^{\flat 9}$ D♭ Maj7 D min7$^{\flat 5}$ G7$^{\sharp 9}$ G♭ Maj7 B♭ min7$^{\flat 5}$ E♭7$^{\flat 9}$ A♭ min7
   c)D Maj7 B min7$^{\flat 5}$ E7$^{\sharp 9}$ F Maj7 A min7 D7$^{\flat 9}$ G min7 B♭ min7 E♭7 A♭ min7 D♭7 G♭ Maj7

Keyboard:

1. Play the preceding written exercises at the keyboard. Observe the minimum of motion used throughout. (Exercises 5a, 5b 5c).
2. Play the four voicings studied in this chapter in all keys as they relate to various chord families. Try to memorize as many as possible.
3. Read lead sheets of jazz tunes at the keyboard and try to use only these four voicings to sound all of the chords. Play the voicings in your right hand and the roots of the chords in your left.
4. Go back and look at the keyboard exercises in Chapter 4 again. Notice how the guidelines of chord connection have been applied and that the voicings used are almost excluseively one of the four studied in this chapter.

Ear-Training:

1. Go back to written Exercise 5 and sing each individual part as a melody moving through the chord progressions. If you have done the exercises correctly, each part should be quite smooth and singable.
2. Listen for a smooth connection of voicings by keyboard players on recordings. Transcribe voicings and play along with the record.
3. Listen for a smooth connection of voicings in jazz band arrangements. Try to follow individual parts (2nd alto, 3rd trombone, 4th trumpet, etc.) through the harmony and listen for melodic smoothness.

## 8. MODES OF THE ASCENDING MELODIC MINOR SCALE

The melodic minor scale is the third traditional form of the minor scale. Actually, it has two forms itself: the ascending melodic minor and the descending melodic minor. Since the descending form is exactly the same scale as the pure minor (Aeolian), it will not be considered here.

The ascending melodic minor is constructed by raising the 6th and 7th scale degrees of a pure minor scale one half-step. The unique quality of this scale is probably due to the fact that the first half of it is minor and the second half is major. In fact, another easy way to construct an ascending melodic minor scale is simply to lower the 3rd scale degree of a major scale one half-step.

By its nature (an alteration of pure minor), the melodic minor scale cannot be conveniently conceived using conventional key signatures. However, unlike the harmonic minor, the modes of the ascending melodic minor do have commonly used names which are closely related to modes of the major scale and can aid in learning them. Example 1 shows the modes of a C (ascending) melodic minor scale written out in order.

Example 1

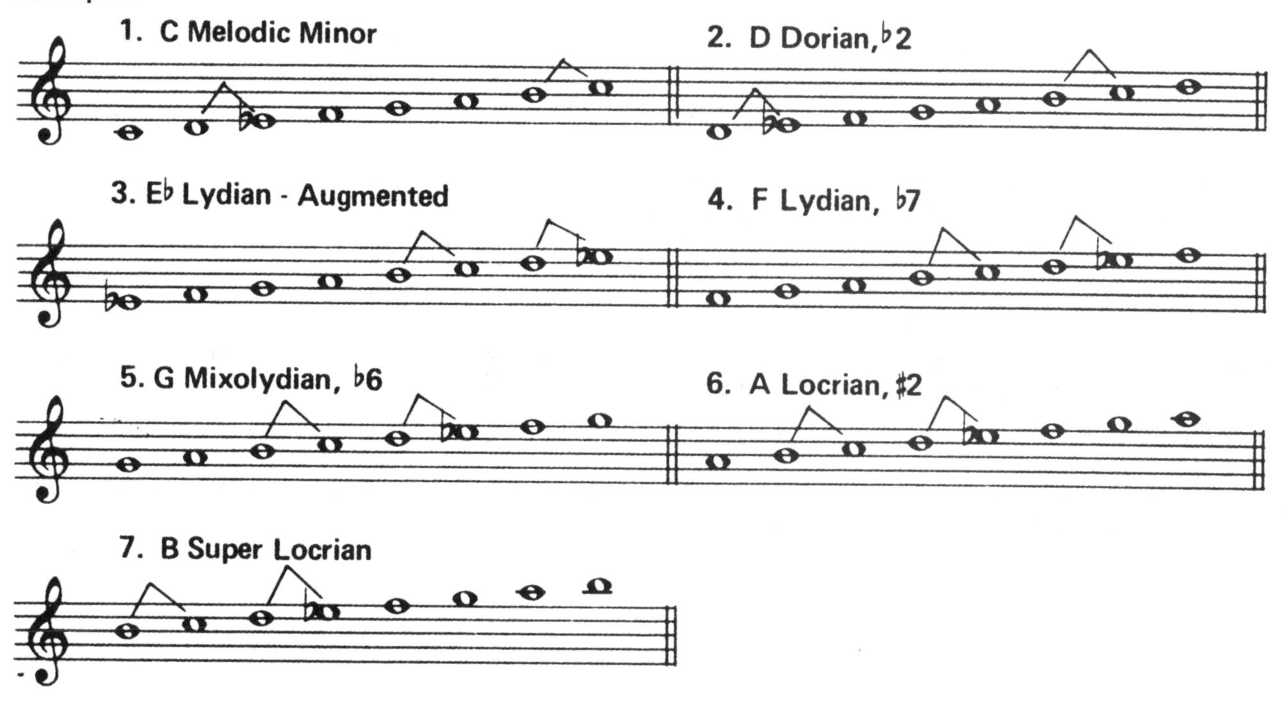


Notice in Example 1 that the location of the two half-steps has been indicated. This can be a definite aid in learning their construction. However, there are two other ways which will probably be easier to use. One is to locate the "parent" key of the desired mode as was suggested with modes of the harmonic minor. For example, if the 4th mode is desired, simply think of the (ascending) melodic minor scale located a perfect 4th below. Example 2 shows all seven modes of the melodic minor scale built on the note C with the "parent" key indicated in parentheses.

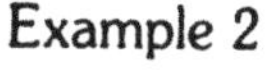
Example 2

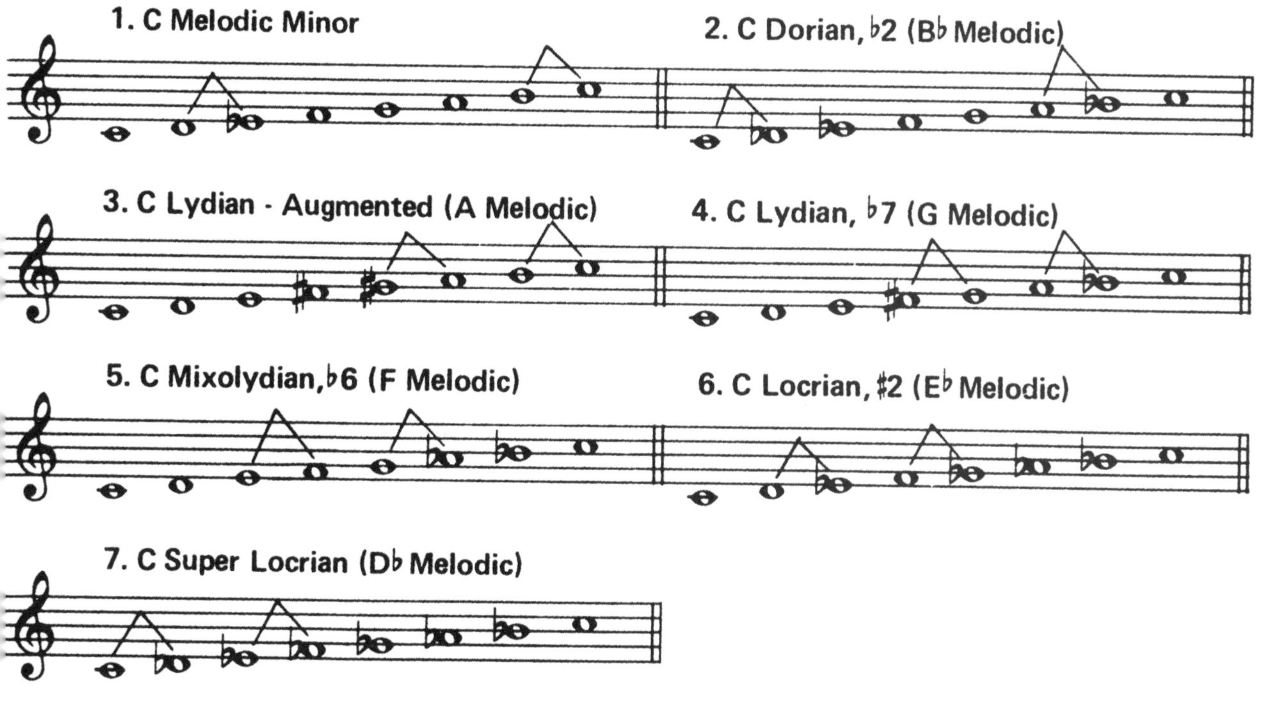

Another way to conceive modes of the melodic minor scale is to relate their construction to similar modes of the major scale. The following chart lists the modes of the melodic minor and shows what alteration is necessary in some major mode to construct it.

| Mode of ascending Melodic Minor | Alteration to a Major Mode |
|---|---|
| 1. Melodic Minor | Major with lowered 3rd |
| 2. Dorian, ♭2 | Dorian with lowered 2nd |
| 3. Lydian-Augmented | Lydian with raised 5th |
| 4. Lydian, ♭7 | Lydian with lowered 7th |
| 5. Mioxlydian, ♭6 | Mixolydian with lowered 6th |
| 6. Locrian, ♯2 | Locrian with raised 2nd |
| 7. Super Locrian | Locrian with lowered 4th |

Chord-Scale Relationships

Just as with modes of the major and harmonic minor scales, each mode of the ascending melodic minor scale has a corresponding diatonic 7th chord. Example 3 shows the diatonic 7th chords of a C ascending melodic minor scale.

Example 3

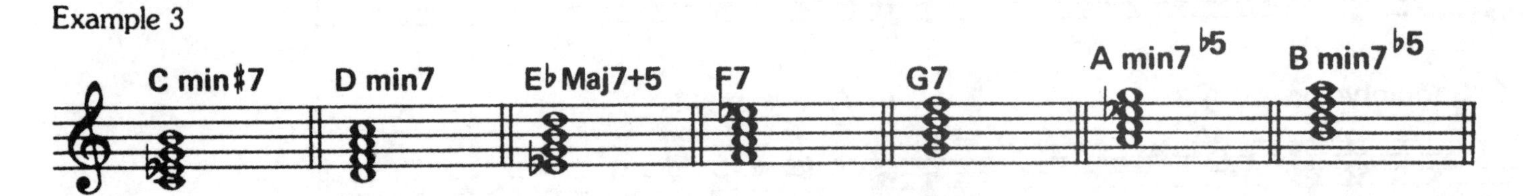


Notice in Example 3 that these chords are similar to the diatonic chords of a harmonic minor scale but differ slightly because of the raised 6th scale step in melodic minor. The II chord is minor instead of half-diminished, the IV chord is dominant instead of minor, the VI chord is half-diminished instead of major, and the VII chord is half-diminished instead of diminished.

The following chart is a summary of the chord-scale relationships of modes of the melodic minor. Notice that, though the diatonic VII chord of a melodic minor scale is half-diminished, the 7th mode (Super Locrian) is usually used with altered dominant chords.

| Mode of Ascending Melodic Minor | Related 7th chord |
|---|---|
| 1. Melodic Minor | Minor, ♯7 |
| 2. Dorian, ♭2 | Minor |
| 3. Lydian-Augmented | Major, ♯5 |
| 4. Lydian, ♭7 | Dominant, ♯11 |
| 5. Mixolydian, ♭6 | Dominant, ♭13 |
| 6. Locrian, ♯2 | Half-diminished |
| 7. Super Locrian | Dominant, altered 5th and 9th |

Like modes of the harmonic minor scale, this group of modes is also very useful in dealing with certain colorations not satisfied by modes of the major scale. An interesting aspect of this group of scales is that there are very few intolerably dissonant tones that require resolution. The modes that do need some attention to dissonant tones are:

| | | |
|---|---|---|
| II | Dorian, ♭2 | The 2nd scale step is dissonant and should resolve to the 1st. |
| III | Lydian-Augmented | The 6th scale step is dissonant and should resolve to the 5th. |
| V | Mixolydian, ♭6 | The 5th or 6th scale steps may be dissonant depending on whether the ♭13 is present or not. Resolve up or down by half-step. |

The modes of melodic minor become very useful in dealing with compositions written since the mid-sixties. Composers such as Chick Corea, Wayne Shorter and Keith Jarrett have made extensive use of harmonies requiring the use of these modes. Analyze many compositions and look for situations that call for some of these specialized colorations!

## STUDY QUESTIONS

1. Name the modes of the ascending melodic minor scale.
2. What is the structure of an ascending melodic minor scale?
3. Can a melodic minor scale be represented by a conventional key signature?
4. What are probably the two best ways to conceive modes of the melodic minor scale?
5. Give the related 7th chord (with alterations) for each mode of the ascending melodic minor scale.
6. Which one of the 7th chords in question 5 differs from the actual diatonic 7th chord of the particular mode?
7. How do the diatonic 7th chords of a melodic minor scale compare with those of a harmonic minor scale?
8. Discuss dissonant tones in the modes and their usual resolutions.

## EXERCISES

Written:

1. In a given key, write out all seven modes of the ascending melodic minor scale. Do not use a key signature but rather locate the sharps or flats in front of the appropriate notes.
2. Write all seven modes of the melodic minor built on the same note. Write the "parent" key above each mode.
3. Write the following modes: F♯ melodic minor; E Dorian, ♭2; G Lydian-Augmented; E♭ Lydian, ♭7; D Mixolydian, ♭6; E Locrian, ♯2; G Super Locrian; B♭ Lydian-Augmented; C♯ Locrian, ♯2; F Super Locrian.
4. Write an eight measure melody in each mode. Be sure to stress important color tones and be careful of the handling of dissonant tones.

Keyboard:

1. Play an ascending melodic minor scale in a given key. Then play all seven modes of it using the same fingering throughout.
2. Play all of the diatonic 7th chords of a given melodic minor scale. Put your thumb on the root of each chord regardless of whether it is a white note or a black note.

Ear-Training:

1. Sing each of the modes of the ascending melodic minor from the root, up an octave and back again.
2. Sing each of the diatonic 7th chords of the melodic minor scale.
3. Working with a friend, practice identification of the modes.
4. Listen for the use of modes of melodic minor in improvised solos on recordings. Transcribe and check by playing with the record.

## 9. POLYCHORD NOMENCLATURE

The term polychord literally means many (poly) chords. In actual practice, a polychord is usually a combination of only two chords which creates a more complex sound. This method of conceiving 13th chords was presented in Chapter 5. But it will be seen in this chapter that chord symbols that look like polychords are commonly used to represent several different things. Example 1 shows four polychord symbols each of which represents a different type of sound.

Example 1

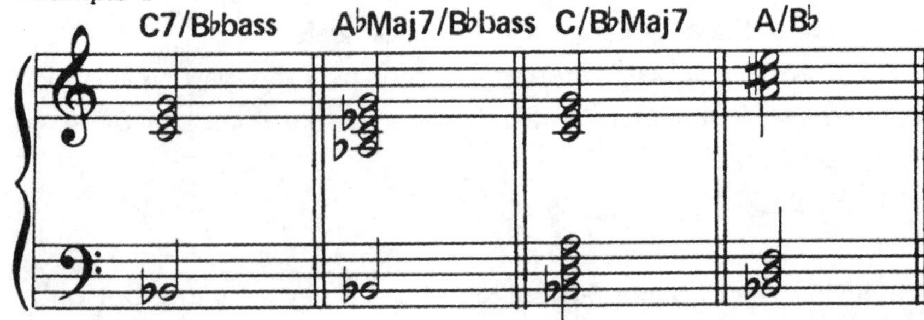


In the previous example, each chord can be explained in the following manner:

a) C7/B♭ bass - A C7 chord with the 7th (B♭ ) in the bass to create a certain musical effect. This chord might be found in the progression C7/B♭ bass to F/A bass where the composer wants to create a particular bass line by the use of inversions.

b) A♭Maj7/B♭ bass - Another way of indicating a B♭13sus4 since the chords tones of the A♭Maj7 represent the 7th, 9th sus4th and 13th of a B♭ chord.

c) C/B♭Maj7 - Another way of indicating a complete B♭Maj13. This insures that 9th, +11th and 13th (optional extensions) will all be present.

d) A/B♭ - A true polychord representing a complex sound of an unconventional nature. This chord could be called a B♭Maj7+9+11 but, since it is a somewhat uncommon chord, it is probably better labeled as a polychord.

A great deal of confusion about polychord nomenclature exists and seems to be due to two main reasons:

1) A polychord symbol sometimes represents two chords and at other times indicates a chord over a particular bass note. Though, in the latter case, the symbol should include the word "bass" or "pedal" (abbreviated ped.), it often does not. However, as will be shown later, this should not cause any confusion as common sense will reveal whether the bottom letter of the symbol is a triad or a single bass note.

2) Some people suggest that a diagonal line in a polychord fraction indicates one thing and a horizontal line indicates another. However, this is not universal and it is the author's opinion that this differentiation only adds to the confusion and is really unnecessary. Again, common sense should make it obvious what the nature of the symbol really is.

In the paragraphs to follow, each aspect of polychord nomenclature will be examined and explained. An attempt will be made to show the logic of interpreting each type of symbol.

### *A Polychord Symbol Indicating an Inversion*

Composers often use inversions to create bass melodies that compliment the actual melody of the song. To be really correct, the word "bass" or "pedal" should follow the bottom letter of the chord symbol if it is a single bass note. To expedite the copying of music in manuscript, these words are often omitted. However, if the bottom letter of the polychord symbol represents a note that is the 3rd, 5th or 7th of the upper chord, it is fairly safe to assume that it is a single bass note used to create an inversion. To be certain, all you have to do is to play the two letters as complete chords on the piano and your ear should tell you if the sound makes sense or not.

Example 2 shows a typical use of polychord nomenclature to indicate a series of inversions. The word "bass" has been intentionally omitted but the stepwise motion of the lower letters of the chord symbols should reveal the reason for the inversions.

Example 2

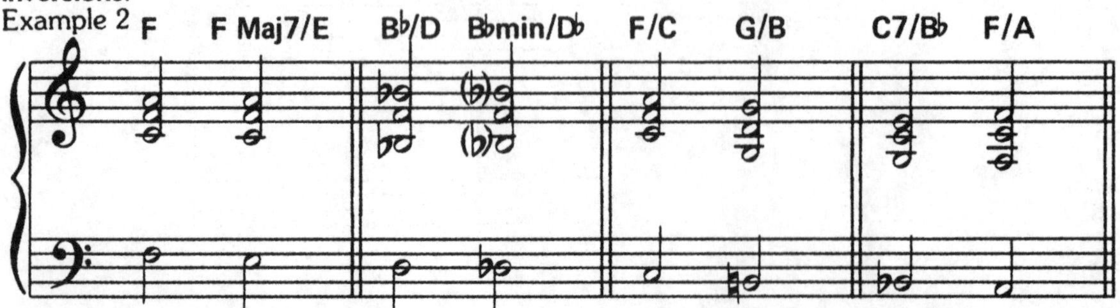


Notice in Example 2 that a typical voicing of the progression has been supplied to show at least one possible realization of the chord symbols. Now go back and play all of the chord symbols in Example 2 as two complete triads and you should discover how unlikely that possibility is.

Remember that only a letter is required to indicate a major triad and that is probably the main reason for confusion. If the bottom chord symbol includes an extension such as a 7 or 9, then it should be pretty obvious that it is representing a complete chord. Another strong clue as to the nature of any polychord symbol will come from an analysis of all the chord tones suggested by both letters of the symbol. If the total sound includes two tones in definite conflict with each other, then the bottom letter is probably not representing a chord but rather a single bass note.

*A Polychord Symbol Indicating a Suspended 4th Chord*

By definition, a suspended 4th chord is one in which the 4th scale step replaces the usual 3rd of the chord. This may be done simply by making that substitution in any chord. However, the same thing can be accomplished by using polychord nomenclature. If the upper chord of the symbol includes the tone which is a perfect 4th above the lower chord root, a suspended sound will be created. Generally the upper chord of the symbol includes other important chord tones in relation to the total sound and the bottom letter is a single bass note which is the root. Example 3 shows several typical polychord symbols which could be used to create a suspended sound on the root C.

Example 3

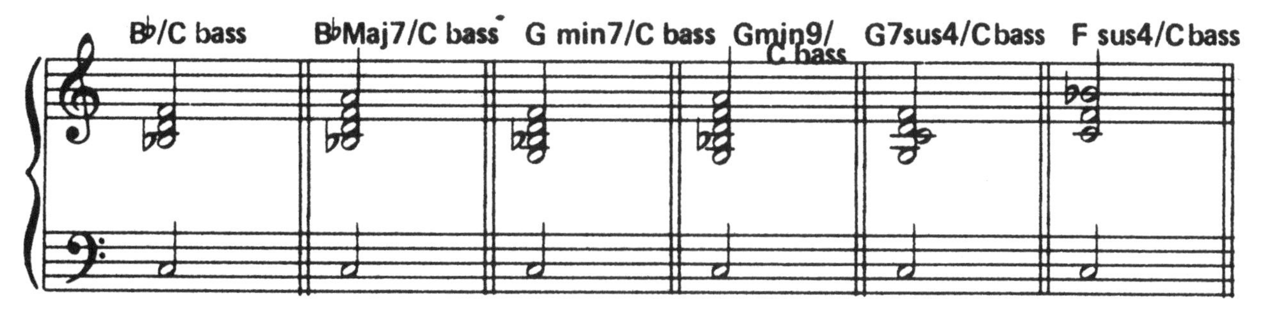


As in chord symbols which indicate inversions, the word "bass" or "pedal" should be included for clarity when indicating a suspended chord. But, as before, common sense would suggest that a chord would probably not have both a major 3rd and a suspended 4th in it. Accordingly, if the upper chord includes the tone which could be a suspended 4th in relation to the bottom letter, it would be safe to assume that the bottom letter is representing a single bass note and the word does not really need to be included. Again, to be certain, check by playing both parts of the chord symbol as complete chords and your ear should tell you the answer quickly! Go back and play the chord symbols in Example 3 as two complete chords and you should, once more, discover how unlikely that sound is.

*A Polychord Symbol Indicating an Extended and/or Altered Chord*

Polychord symbols are an extremely convenient way of describing complex sounds in a very simple way. Besides making it easy to construct complete 13th chords, polychord symbols facilitate the notation of many colorful and complex harmonies. Example 4 shows some typical polychords that might occur in relation to major, minor and dominant family chords.

Example 4

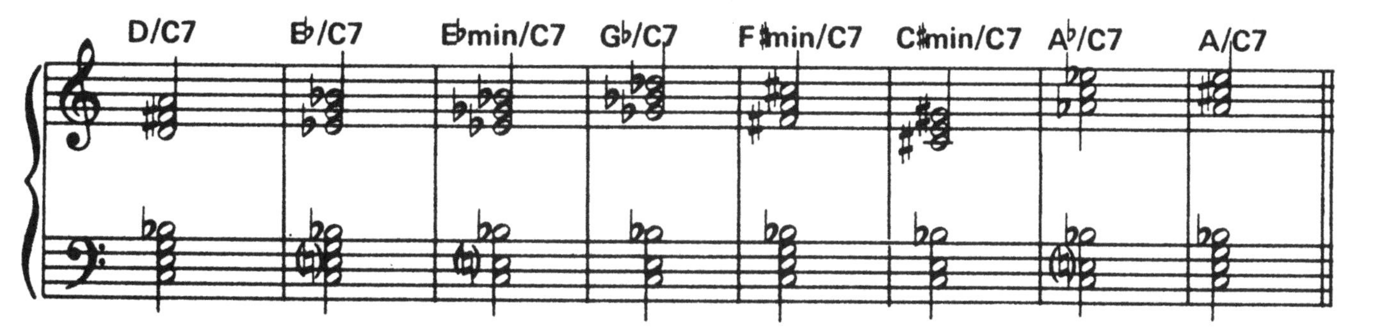


Even though many of the chords in Example 4 are rather conventional, a polychord treatment (voicing) of them produces a special kind of musical effect. To insure this kind of effect, the two parts of the chord must be kept separate from each other just as the slash in the fraction separates them. For example, a writer might have trumpets play the upper chord and trombones play the lower chord or a pianist might play one chord in his right hand and the other in his left. This is merely one kind of treatment of harmony and not necessarily the best.

Notice also in Example 4 that the 5th has been omitted from the bottom chord in some cases. This is because the upper chord includes a tone which is an altered 5th in relation to the total sound and the unaltered 5th would tend to create a clash if it were included. If the sound of a ♯11 or ♭13 is desired, then the natural 5th might be included.

*A Polychord Symbol Indicating an Unconventional Sonority*

Some sonorities can be created with polychords that are either unconventional or are extremely difficult to represent with a conventional chord symbol. Example 5 shows some polychords which would probably not be commonly used in most musical situations. Though some of these chords could be indicated by a normal chord symbol with alterations, it is much easier to use a polychord.

Example 5

Notice in the previous example such things as a major 7th chord with a ♯9, a chord with both a major 7th and a minor 7th in it, and a chord with both a major 3rd and a natural 4th. These are unusual sonorities but are certainly possible in the context of some types of compositions. Example 6 shows what might truly be called polychords since they are comprised of not just two but three different chords.

Example 6

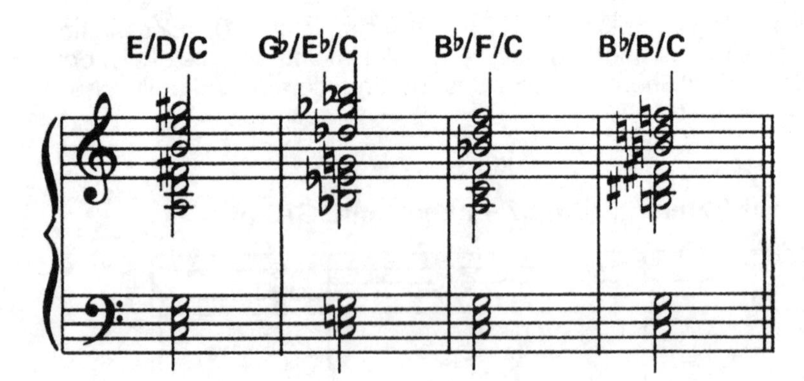


To summarize, it is important to remember that polychord nomenclature is commonly used to represent any of the following:

1) An inversion of a chord.
2) A suspended 4th chord.
3) An extended and/or altered chord.
4) An unconventional sonority.

STUDY QUESTIONS

1. What does the term polychord mean literally and in actual practice?
2. What are the two main reasons that confusion exists about polychords?
3. How can you tell if a polychord symbol indicates an inversion?
4. How can you recognize a polychord symbol which indicates a suspended chord?
5. What word should be included for clarity if the bottom letter of a polychord is supposed to represent a single note?
6. In voicing polychords, what must be done to retain the polychord sound?
7. Why is the 5th of the bottom chord sometimes omitted in altered polychords and when might it be included?
8. What is the advantage of using polychords to create unusual sonorities?
9. What are the four ways in which polychord nomenclature is commonly used?

# EXERCISES

Written:

1. Convert the polychord symbols in Examples 3 and 4 to conventional chords symbols. For example, B♭/C bass = C9 sus4 or D/C Ma7 = C Ma13.
2. Convert the following normal chord symbols to polychord symbols: Dmin11, B♭ma9+11, G13♭9, Emin13, E Ma13, F7-5-9, E♭Ma7+5, Ami9♯7, D7+5+9, B7+9, G9sus4, B♭7sus4.
3. Analyze the Polychords in Examples 3 and 4 and create general formulas for building them in any key. Use the following format:

   a) B♭/C bass = C9sus4 = a major triad a whole step below over bass note.

   b)D/CMa7 = C Ma13 = a major triad a whole step above a major 7th.
4. Transpose various polychord formulas to all keys and write both the chord symbols and the correct notes on the staff.

Keyboard:

1. Play the polychords in Examples 3, 4 and 5 at the piano. Keep the upper chord in the right hand and the lower chord or bass note in the left hand. Try inverting either or both of the chords to acheive different voicings of the same chord. Example 7 shows several different voicings of an E♭/C chord.

Example 7

2. Using the formulas developed in written Exercise 3, play various types of polychords and transpose to all keys.

Ear-Training:

1. Working with another person, practice identification of typical polychords including suspended chords and inversions. Always test by singing up through the chord.
2. Listen for the use of polychordal voicings by writers or keyboard players on recordings. Transcribe specific voicings and analyze.
3. Listen for improvisers on recordings to play melodic ideas based on the upper chord of a polychord. Transcribe and test by playing along with the record.
4. Practice singing the individual chords of various types of polychords as you play them at the piano.

## 10. SYMMETRICAL ALTERED SCALES

Symmetrical scales are those which have a regular, recurring structure of intervals. Other scales studied in previous chapters all include 2 or 3 half steps which occur at certain points in the scales. Symmetrical scales may be composed entirely of whole steps or half steps or else an equal number of certain intervals. Also, this group of scales relates to chords which have altered chord tones so the label *symmetrical altered scales* seems appropriate.

The scales to be studied in this chapter are listed below with a description of their structure.

| | |
|---|---|
| 1. Chromatic | ½ ½ ½ ½ ½ ½ ½ ½ ½ ½ ½ ½ |
| 2. Whole Tone | w w w w w w |
| 3. w-½ Diminished | w ½ w ½ w ½ w ½ |
| 4. ½-w Diminshed | ½ w ½ w ½ w ½ w |
| 5. Augmented | +2nd ½ +2nd ½ +2nd ½ |

The previous chart should make apparent the symmetrical nature of these scales. Example 1 shows each of the scales built on the note C.

Example 1

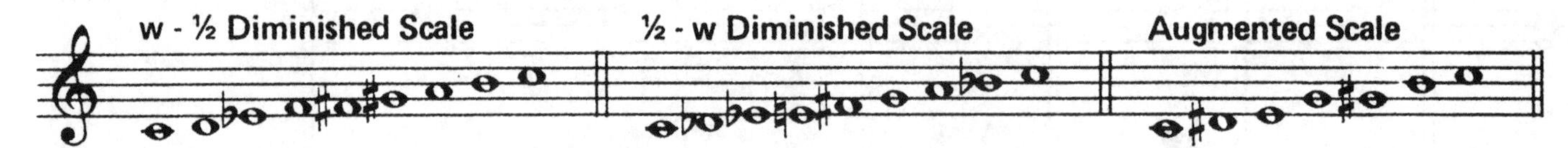


Since each of the scales in this chapter (with the exception of the two diminished scales) is fairly unique, they will be discussed separately as to their structure, diatonic chords, and chord-scale relationships.

### The Chromatic Scale

This scale is constructed exclusively of half steps. As a result, there is only one chromatic scale (sound) which may begin on any tone. Example 2 shows the chromatic scale as it would be typically notated in ascending or descending forms

Example 2

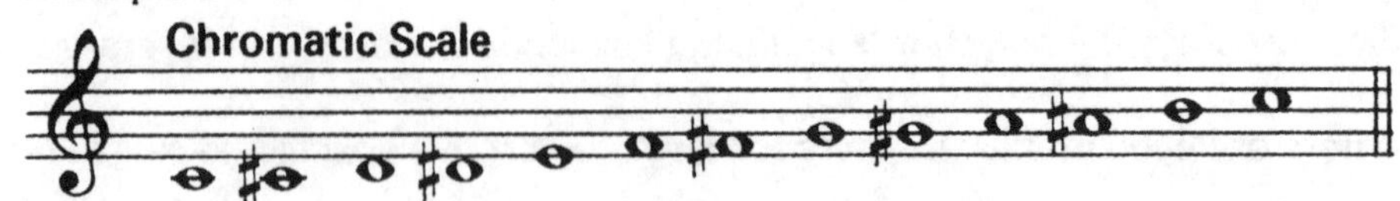

The chromatic scale may be used with any chord type with any combination of alterations. Naturally, some scale tones will always be dissonant to the harmony and have a strong tendency to resolve. This resolution will probably be either up or down by a half step to the nearest chord tone.

Chromatic motion can create excitement if used sparingly. If more than 4 or 5 successive chromatic scale steps are used, the musical style may become rather "cocktailish" in character. This is because of the proliferation of"rippling" chromatic runs found in much commercial music. However, short chromatic groups of notes can generate melodic energy and certainly should not be avoided.

Because of its nature, the chromatic scale contains all of the conventional triads and seventh chords in all keys. Thus, it would be tedious and unnecessary to list them all.

### The Whole Tone Scale

The *Whole Tone Scale* is constructed exclusively of whole steps, six in all. As a result, there are only two different sounding whole tone scales which are located a half step away from each other. Each of the two scales may be reinterpreted as six different scales enharmonically. Example 3 shows the two whole tone scales built on C and C♯.

Example 3

Notice in the previous example that a whole tone scale omits one letter of the musical alphabet in its spelling. This is because it is a six-tone scale. Therefore, a diminished 3rd must occur somewhere in the structure. This results in a rather strange looking scale which always appears to have a skip in it even though it is built entirely of whole steps!

The whole tone scale includes six augmented triads and six dominant seventh chords which have altered 5ths. Thus, each of the two whole tone scales accommodates six of the twelve keys. Normally, the whole tone scale is used with a dominant 7th chord which has either a raised or lowered 5th or both. It can also be used with an augmented triad that has a dominant function (one which resolves upward by half-step or down a 5th). It is important to remember that this scale includes a natural 2nd (9th) scale step and so it is not a good choice if an altered 9th is present in the harmony.

## Diminished Scales

Diminished scales are constructed of 4 whole steps and 4 half steps in regular alternation. A scale may begin either with a half step or a whole step depending on its application. There are only three different sounding scales each of which serves four keys. Essentially, a diminished scale is an eight tone scale which starts over again on every other note. Example 4 shows the three different sounding diminished scales.

Example 4

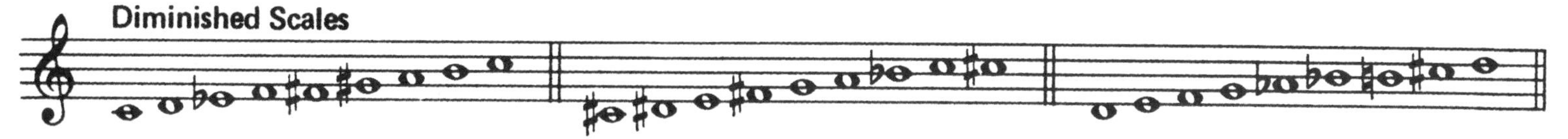


Notice in the previous example that one letter of the musical alphabet must be repeated to construct a diminished scale. The repeated letter may occur at any convenient point in the scale.

A diminished scale includes 4 minor triads, 4 major triads, 8 diminished triads, 4 minor 7th chords, 4 dominant 7th chords, and 8 diminished 7th chords. The scale is not usually a good choice for minor chords even though they appear in the scale. There are other scales that are more appropriate to a true minor sound. Normally, diminished scales are used with diminished 7th chords or dominant 7th chords with altered 9ths.

Example 5 shows a diminished scale which begins with a half step. Notice that all of the scale tones can be accounted for as either a chord tone or altered chord tone in the accompanying dominant 7th.

Example 5

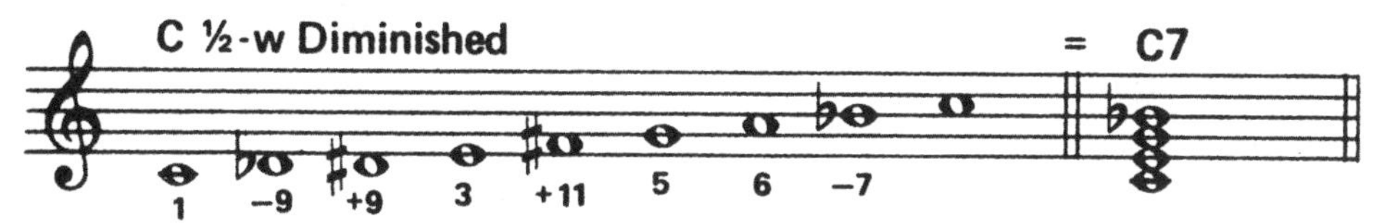


If the diminished scale which begins with a whole step were used with a dominant 7th, it would be very dissonant since it includes the tone a major 7th above the root.

Example 6 shows a diminished scale which begins with a whole step used with a diminished 7th chord. Notice the scale includes all the tones of the diminished 7th plus a note which is a whole step above each chord tone.

Example 6

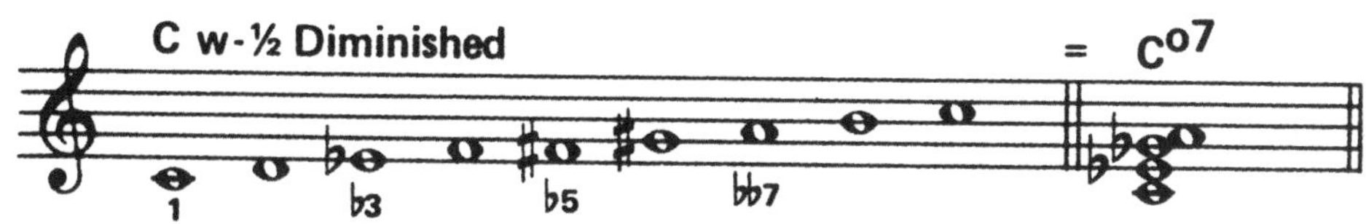


Normally, when tones are added to a diminished 7th chord, they are tones which are a whole step above any chord tone since these are more consonant than tones a half step above. Therefore, the whole step-half step scale is usually chosen for a diminished 7th chord. In some instances, the half step-whole step scale may be used for a diminished chord in a descending melodic passage.

The augmented scale is constructed of alternating augmented 2nds (minor 3rds) and half steps. There are only four different sounding augmented scales each of which relates to three keys. Example 7 shows the four augmented scales.

Example 7

Notice in the previous example that, like the whole tone scale, the augmented scale is a six tone scale which omits one letter of the musical alphabet. The letter may be omitted at any convenient point in the scale.

The augmented scale includes 3 minor triads, 3 major triads, 6 augmented triads, 3 minor♯7 chords, 3 major 7th chords, and 3 augmented major 7th chords. Normally it is only used with augmented chords though it could be used with major chords. Example 8 shows the augmented scale used with an augmented major 7th chord. Notice that the 2nd and 4th scale steps tend to act like non-harmonic approach tones.

Example 8

Because of their nature, symmetrical altered scales are often used to generate ascending or descending melodic patterns which move through the scales in a regular manner. Example 9 shows some typical patterns generated by each scale form.

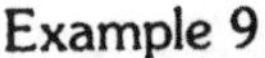
Example 9

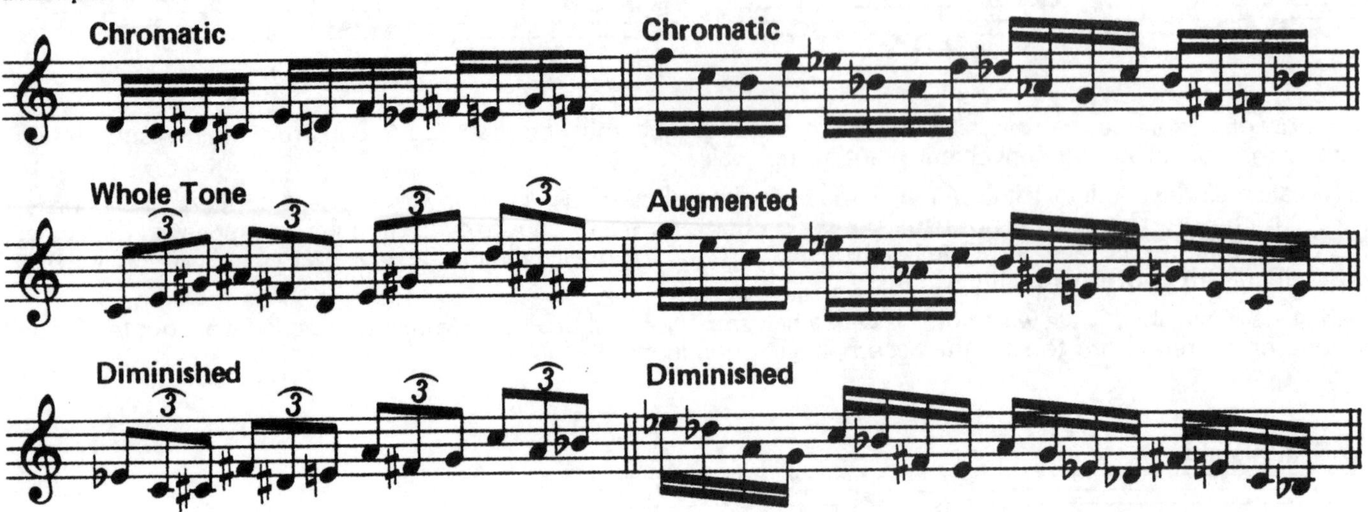


## STUDY QUESTIONS

1. Why are the scales studied in this chapter called symmetrical altered scales?
2. Give the chord-scale relationships for each of the scales.
3. What is a problem with overuse of the chromatic scale?
4. Tell what kinds of triads and seventh chords are included in each of the symmetrical altered scales.
5. What is unusual about the spelling of symmetrical altered sclaes?
6. Why might a diminished scale begin with either a half step or a whole step?
7. Are symmetrical scales used to generate melodic patterns? If so, why?

## EXERCISES

Written:

1. Write out the F and G♭ whole tone scales.
2. Write out the F♯, G and G♯ whole step-half step diminished scales.
3. Write out the A, B♭ and B half step-whole step diminished scales.
4. Write out the A♭, A, B♭ and B augmented scales.
5. Write an eight measure melody using each of the five symmetrical scales.

Keyboard:

1. Play each of the symmetrical scales from a given pitch. Keep your thumb off of black notes but notice that there is more than one possible place to cross over or under.
2. Play a particular symmetrical scale and then locate all of the diatonic triads and seventh chords. Play these chords and put your thumb on the root of each regardless of whether it is a black note or white note.

Ear-Training

1. Sing each of the symmetrical altered scales while playing the seventh chord to which it relates in root position. Be sure to raise the 5th of the seventh chord for a whole tone or augmented scale.
2. Working with another person, practice identification of the symmetrical altered scales. The person playing the scale should always cover a span of eight tones regardless of the structure of the scale.
3. Listen for the use of symmetrical scales in improvised solos on recordings. Transcribe and check by playing with the record.

# 11. ADVANCED SUBSTITUTION AND FUNCTION

Before proceeding with this chapter, it may be helpful to go back and review Chapter 4. At the very least, a brief restatement of basic chord functions seems appropriate at this point. Whereas the various functions were grouped by major or minor keys in chapter 4, the following chart organizes all of the normal functions by chord family:

| Chord Family | Normal Function(s) |
|---|---|
| Major 7th | I or IV in major<br>III or VI in minor |
| Minor 7th | I or IV in minor<br>II, III or VI in major |
| Dominant 7th | V in major<br>V or VII in minor |
| Half-Diminished | II or ♯VI in minor<br>VII in major |
| Diminished 7th | ♯VII in minor |

## Borrowed Chords

As was seen in the previous chart, each of the 5 main types of chords has places where it normally occurs in either a major or minor key. However, chords are often "borrowed" from a minor key to be used in major or vice versa. When this occurs, a chord is simply taken from the parallel key. For example, a chord might be borrowed from C minor to be used in C major.

When chords are borrowed, an adjustment of the Roman Numeral symbol may be necessary. The following chart shows chords which are commonly borrowed for use either in a major or minor key and the correct label for each:

| Label in major key | Label in minor key |
|---|---|
| II min7 | II min7 * |
| II min7-5 * | II min7-5 |
| ♭III maj7 * | III maj7 |
| IV min7 * | IV min7 |
| ♭VI maj7 * | VI maj7 |
| ♭VII dom7 * | VII dom7 |
| VII dim7 * | ♯VII dim7 |

* Borrowed chords

## Secondary Dominants

Normally dominant 7th chords occur as V chords in major or minor keys. Since jazz progressions change key a great deal, this accounts for the majority of dominant 7ths. However, in some cases, dominant 7ths will occur on other scale degrees to increase the harmonic drive toward certain chords of a single key. Though a feeling of V to I may be present, no actual change of key has taken place in such instances. The following chart shows the usual location of secondary dominants (in either major or minor) and their normal resolutions:

| Location of Secondary Dominant | Normal Resolution(s) |
|---|---|
| I 7 | IV |
| ♭II 7 * | I |
| II 7 | V or ♭II |
| ♭III 7 * | ♭VI or II |
| III 7 | VI or ♭III |
| ♭VI 7 * | ♭II or V |
| VI 7 | II or ♭VI |
| ♭VII 7 * | ♭III or VI |
| VII 7 | III or ♭VII |

*Tri-tone substitutions

Notice in the previous chart that dominant 7ths can commonly resolve either down a half step or down a perfect 5th. Therefore, when stronger harmonic drive is desired, virtually any chord may be approached from either a half step above or a perfect 5th above. Secondary dominants are particularly common in turn-around progressions such as Ima7-VI7-IImi7-V7-Ima7 or Ima7-♭III7-II7-♭II7-Ima7.

A diminished 7th chord (which is often a substitute for a dominant 7th) can also function in a secondary capacity. In such cases, it is simply constructed on the "leading tone" of the chord to follow and resolves normally up a half step. For example, secondary diminished chords might occur in progressions such as ♯Idim7-IImi7, IIIdim7-IVma7, or ♯IVdim7-V7. It would be a good idea to review the discussion of the diminished 7th in Chapter 4 since secondary applications can be confusing in the same way that the normal function can be.

## Dual Functions

It has been seen that each chord type (with the exception of the diminished 7th) has more than one common function. This ability of a chord to function in more than one way allows the composer to make subtle, smooth changes of key rather than an abrupt, sudden jump into another key. In traditional harmony, a chord which could function in both of two adjacent keys was called a pivot chord for the change of key. This created what was called a common chord modulation as opposed to a direct modulation.

In Chapter 4, it was shown how many jazz progressions are based on a series of direct modulations from key to key with no common chord found between keys. In this chapter, we will see some interesting uses of dual functions (pivot chords) in moving from key to key. The following example shows a progression that moves from the key of E♭ to the key of Dmi. The modulation is performed smoothly through the use of Gmi7 as a dual function since it is a IIImi7 in E♭ and a IVmi7 in Dmi.

Example 1

E♭: I VI II V III

E♭ Maj7 C min7 F min7 B♭7 G min7 E min7$^{-5}$ A7$^{-9}$ D min7

D min: IV II V I

Notice in the previous example that, by bracketing the keys above and below, the dual function of the Gmi7 becomes very obvious. The following example shows a series of rapid key changes always using a dual function (pivot chord) to move from key to key.

Example 2

E♭: II V III A min: VI II V I

F min7 B♭7 G min7 C7 F Maj7 B min7$^{-5}$ E7$^{-9}$ A min7 F♯ min7$^{-5}$ B7$^{-9}$ E min7

F: II V I E min: IV II V I

Another factor which adds to the subtlety of key changes is the use of borrowed chords or secondary dominants in a dual function. The following example moves from key to key by means of a pivot chord which functions as either a borrowed chord or a secondary dominant in one of the two adjacent keys.

Example 3

D min: II V I C♯: ♭VI V I ♭VII F♯: V I

E min7$^{-5}$ A7$^{-9}$ D min7 E7 A Maj7 G♯7 C♯ Maj7 B7 E Maj7 C♯7 F♯ Maj7

A: IV min V I E: V I VI

Basically, the procedure to follow in analyzing modulations is as follows:

1) Look for common functions which suggest a certain key. These will usually be chords which could be analyzed as I, II, IV or V in either a major or minor key.
2) Bracket as many chords as can be accounted for in the key. These might include borrowed or secondary chords.
3) When you come to a chord that cannot be explained in the previous key, repeat the procedure in No. 1.
4) Once the new key is determined, look back at the last chord within the previous key bracket to figure out its dual function in the new key. If there is no explanation for that chord in the new key, then a direct modulation has taken place.

## Chord Quality Changes

In addition to using borrowed or secondary chords, it is also possible to change the quality of certain chords to create a different musical effect. For example, the III chord in a major key is normally a minor 7th chord. But by changing the quality of the chord, other key feelings and stronger or weaker progressions can be suggested. The following chart shows an Emi7 which is a III chord in C major and indicates other keys that might be hinted at by changing the quality of the chord.

| Chord | Function |
|---|---|
| Emi7 | III in C major |
| Ema7 | I in E Major |
| E7 | V in A Major or ♭II in E♭ Major |
| Emi7♭5 | II in D minor |
| Edim7 | VII in F minor |

Changing the quality of chords is especially useful in somewhat free harmonizations of melodies to create unexpected modulations and cadences. Actually, quality changes can be another form of direct modulation in that no dual function has been employed.

## Tri-tone Substitutions

The basic principle of tri-tone substitutions is very simple. Two dominant 7th chords whose roots are a tri-tone (3 whole steps) apart substitute for each other. One of the reasons for this is that the two 7th chords have the same color tones (3rd and 7th) in common. The 3rd of one of the chords is the 7th of the other and vice versa. Example 4 shows a pair of tri-tone substitutes.

Example 4

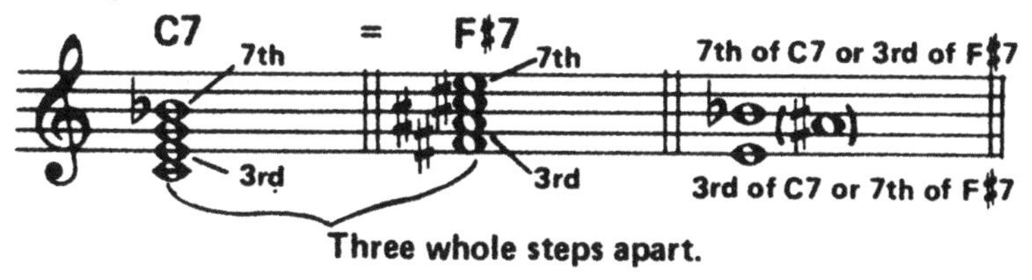


This is a specialized form of common tone substitution which only applies to dominant 7th chords. Other types of chords whose roots are located a tri-tone apart do not share the same color tones. In some cases, however, quality changes are combined with tri-tone substitutions to create interesting effects.

Another reason that tri-tone substitutions of dominant 7ths are possible is because of the resolution of the two color tones which themselves form the interval of a tri-tone. Traditionally, the tri-tone found between the 3rd and 7th of a dominant chord may resolve one of two ways. If it appears as an augmented 4th, it expands (augments) in its resolution. If it appears as a diminished 5th, it contracts (diminishes) in its resolution. The following example shows the 3rd and 7th of a C7 in both normal resolutions to an F major chord.

Example 5

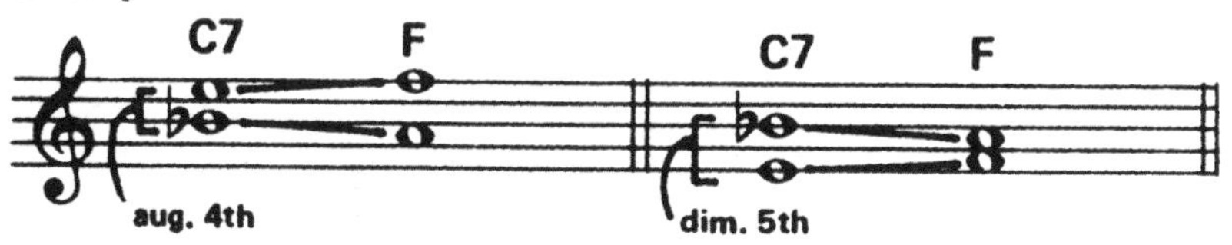


Now, if the B♭ is respelled enharmonically as A♯, both normal resolutions of the 3rd and 7th of an F♯7 can be shown as they would move to a B major chord.

Example 6

It should be apparent by now that, since the same tri-tone respelled enharmonically can resolve to either an F or B chord, the C7 and the F♯7 can both resolve to either key. The example below shows this flexibility:

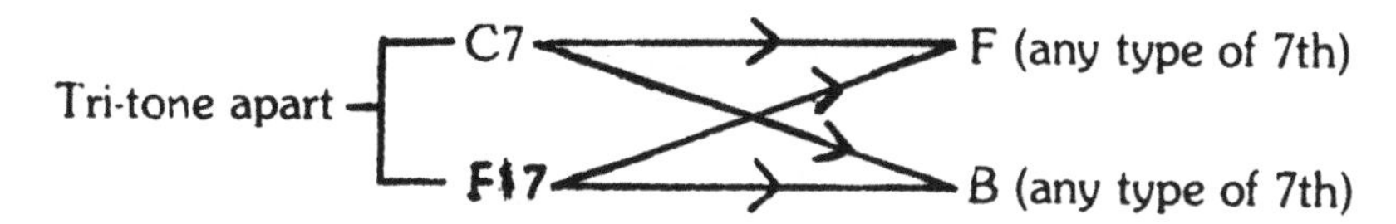


There are only 6 pairs of dominant 7ths which are tri-tone substitutes for each other: C7 and F♯7(G♭7), C♯7(D♭7) and G7, D7 and A♭7, E♭7 and A7, E7 and B♭7, and F7 and B7. Learn to think of each of these pairs as a single chord since they are, in fact, the same basic sound with a choice of two different bass notes. Any time a dominant 7th occurs in a chord progression, there is a good chance that a tri-tone substitution could be made depending on the musical effect desired.

Often, the exact same voicing of the original dominant chord can be retained with only the root being changed. This is useful information to a writer or keyboard player (including guitar and vibes). There are many formulas that apply to tri-tone substitutions in situations where the root is the only tone changed. Example 7 shows some of these formulas.

Example 7

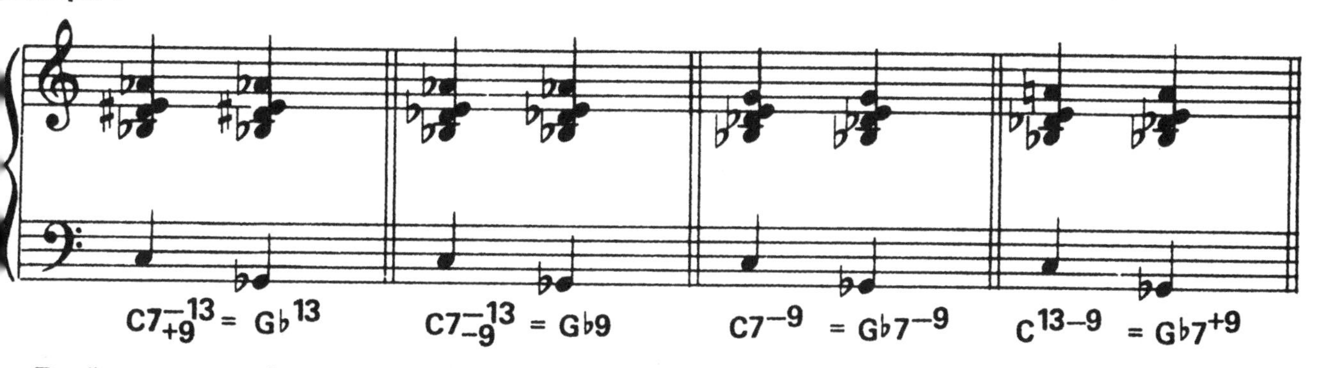


Finally, a tri-tone substitution in analysis only makes an effective dual function in a modulation. For example, a G7 which is V in C major is redefined as a ♭II in G♭ Major and resolves accordingly. No actual tri-tone substitution has taken place, but it has been reassigned a function a tri-tone away from its original one. In traditional harmony, the German 6th chord was used similarly.

## Melody Harmonization

Once a solid understanding of chord function and substitution is gained, melody harmonization can become an extremely entertaining pastime. A melody can be harmonized using only diatonic chords which function completely normally within a single key. Or the same melody can be harmonized using frequent modulations, borrowed chords, secondary dominants, dual functions, quality changes and tri-tone substitutions. Sometimes substitutions may be made which involve chords that have only the original melody note in common. If it is based on a strong function, even a very unlikely progression can sound very convincing. Sometimes a melody written in one key may be harmonized in an entirely different key with good results. The following examples show a traditional melody harmonized freely with few chord roots in common with the original harmony.

Example 8

Notice in the previous examples that this type of free harmonization can add a lot of interest to melodies that are otherwise simple and lacking in harmonic complexity. Folk tunes or hymn tunes that can be harmonized with only the I, IV and V chords are especially good resources for practice exercises. Regular experimentation will lead to the discovery of many interesting possibilities. In the beginning, melodies that move mainly in a stepwise motion and which are comprised of mostly quarter notes and half notes are the best choice.

## STUDY QUESTIONS

1. What are the normal functions of the 5 types of 7th chords?
2. Explain what borrowed chords are and how they are used.
3. What are secondary dominant or secondary diminished chords?
4. What is meant by the term dual function?
5. What is the difference between a direct modulation and one which involves the use of a pivot chord?
6. What steps should you follow in analyzing modulations?
7. What is the effect of changing the quality of a chord?
8. Explain the principle of tri-tone substitutions including the reasons why they are possible.
9. What are some of the interesting possibilities for the free harmonization of melodies?

## EXERCISES

Written:

1. Analyze the following progressions. Bracket and label keys alternately above and below the progression. Two adjacent keys should always share one chord in common which has a dual function in both keys. The pivot chord may be a normal diatonic chord, a borrowed chord or a secondary dominant.
   a) Cma7 Emi7 Fma7 G7 Ama7 F♯mi7 Bmi7 C♯7 F♯ma7 F7 B♭mi7 Gmi7-5 C7 Fmi7 B♭7 E♭ma7 A♭ma7 Dmi7 G7 Cma7
   b) Dmi7-5 G7 Cmi7 F7 B♭ma7 F7 Ema7 G♯mi7 C♯mi7 F♯7 Bma7 B♭7 E♭ma7 Dmi7-5 Gmi7-5 C7 Bmi7 Gma7 F♯7 A♭ma7
   c) A♭mi7 D♭7 G♭ma7 Fmi7 B♭7 E♭ma7 Cmi7 D7 Gma7 Emi7 Ami7 A♭7 D♭ma7 Cmi7-5 F7 B♭ma7 A♭7 Gma7 A7 Dma7
2. Compose an original progression 15 to 20 chords in length. Move to a new key every 3 or 4 chords using dual function pivot chords. Try to use borrowed chords, secondary cominants and tri-tone substitutions.
3. Harmonize a simple melody which is 8 to 16 measures long. Use modulations even though the melody does not change keys and change the quality of some chords to create a different effect.

Keyboard:

1. Play the progressions supplied or created in the written exercises at the piano. Play the root of each chord in the left hand and play voicings studied in Chapter 7 in the right. Be sure to follow the guidelines for connecting voicings smoothly.
2. Experiment with various kinds of altered dominant 7th chord voicings. Play the voicing in the right hand and play first the original root and then the root a tri-tone away in the left hand. If the voicing does not sound good with the root change, adjust it so it sounds good with either bass note. Also play the formulas in Example 7 and transpose to other keys.

Ear-training:

1. Transcribe complex harmony from recordings. Always listen for the notes played by the bass as well as specific voicings used by the pianist or guitar player. Try to locate a reliable lead sheet against which to check your version. Analyze the progression and learn to identify certain functions in other recordings.
2. Working with another person, practice identification of short progressions using borrowed and secondary chords as well as tri-tone substitutions.

## 12. PENTATONIC AND BLUES SCALES

Though everyone is familiar with the sound of playing on only the black notes of the piano, not everyone realizes that they form a pure pentatonic scale. A pentatonic scale is simply a five (penta-) tone (tonic) scale. Generally the five tones divide the octave fairly evenly with no single large interval present. Though any arrangement of five tones within the octave forms a pentatonic scale, certain structures are more commonly used.

### Major Pentatonic

Again referring to the black notes of the piano, we can easily visualize the structure of a pentatonic scale. If the scale begins on G♭, it is a G♭ major pentatonic. That is, it consists of the 1st, 2nd, 3rd, 5th and 6th tones of a G♭ major scale. Thus, if we omit the 4th and 7th tones of any major scale, a major pentatonic will remain. Example 1 shows a G♭ major scale (complete) and with the two notes omitted to form a major pentatonic scale.

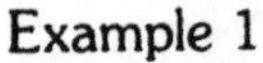
Example 1

Another way to conceive the major pentatonic scale is by its interval structure which is as follows: ma2, ma2, mi3, ma2, mi3. Example 2 shows this interval structure on the same G    major pentatonic as before.

Example 2

Though this scale is derived from a major scale, it has several applications which relate to different families of chords. The major pentatonic structure (1, 2, 3, 5, 6 of a major scale) may be superimposed in several different places on major, minor or dominant chords. The following chart shows some common uses of the scale.

| Chord Type | Location of Pentatonic Root |
|---|---|
| Maj | Built of root of chord |
| Maj9 | Built on 5th of chord |
| Maj13 | Built on 9th of chord |
| min 7 | Built on 3rd of chord |
| min9 | Built on 7th of chord |
| min 13 | Built on 4th of chord |
| Dom7 | Built on root of chord |
| Dom7sus4 | Built on 4th or 7th of chord |
| Dom 7+9 | Built on +9th of chord |
| Dom7+5+9 | Built on tri-tone away |

From the previous chart, it should be apparent that there are many useful applications of pentatonic scales. By superimposing the scale at different points on a chord, one is, in effect, using different modes of the scale. However, this approach is much simpler than learning several different modes in all keys. Also, by superimposing a pentatonic scale at a certain point, it is an excellent way of stressing only certain chord tones for a particular musical effect. An analysis of which chord tones or altered chord tones are stressed by a particular superimposition of a pentatonic will lead to a better understanding of its uses.

### Minor Pentatonic

Many people consider the major pentatonic structure as the only type of pentatonic scale. However, possibly from the conditioning of our major-minor tonal system, some people also hear a minor form of pentatonic as well. In reality, it is a mode of the major pentatonic just as the pure minor is a mode of the major scale. In fact, it is found in the same relationship as a relative minor scale, a minor 3rd below the major pentatonic. Looking once more at the black notes of the piano, the minor pentatonic is found to begin on E♭. The scale consists of the 1st, 3rd, 4th, 5th and 7th tones of an E♭ pure minor scale. Thus, if we omit the 2nd and 6th tones of any pure minor scale, a minor pentatonic will remain. Example 3 shows an E♭ pure minor scale (complete) and with the two tones omitted to form an E♭ minor pentatonic.

Example 3

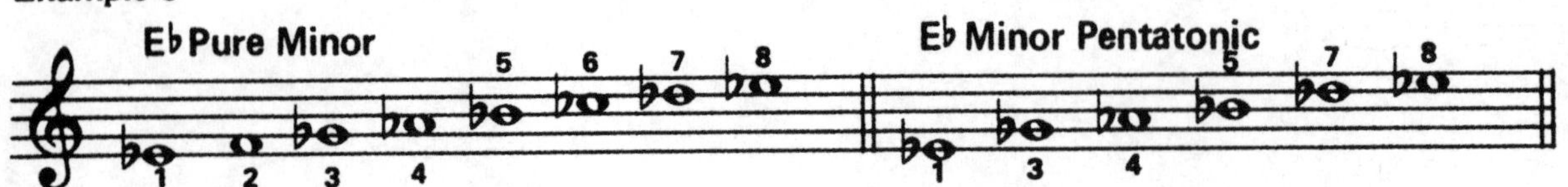

Another way to conceive the minor pentatonic scale is by its interval structure which is: mi3, ma2, ma2, mi3, ma2. Example 4 shows this interval structure on an E♭ minor pentatonic scale.

Example 4

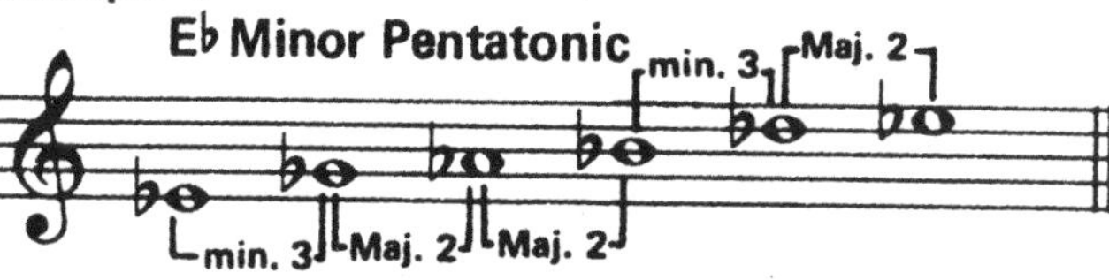


Like the major form, the minor pentatonic can be superimposed in various positions on different chord types. Instead of creating another chart of minor pentatonic root locations, suffice to say that the minor pentatonic would be found on the chord tone a minor 3rd below the location of a major pentatonic on any chord. A logical, simplified summary of pentatonic scale superimpositions is presented later in the chapter.

## Synthetic Pentatonics

At the beginning of the chapter, the black notes of the piano were described as a "pure" pentatonic scale. Whether "pure" or not, the major or minor pentatonic scale is the form one normally thinks of as being a pentatonic scale. However, neither the major nor the minor pentatonic structure is applicable to certain chord types or altered situations. In such cases, either the major or minor form may be adjusted slightly to accommodate the proper sound.

Example 5 shows a synthetic pentatonic used in relation to a Cmaj7+5. This is actually an E major pentatonic with the 5th scale tone (C♯) lowered a half step.

Example 5

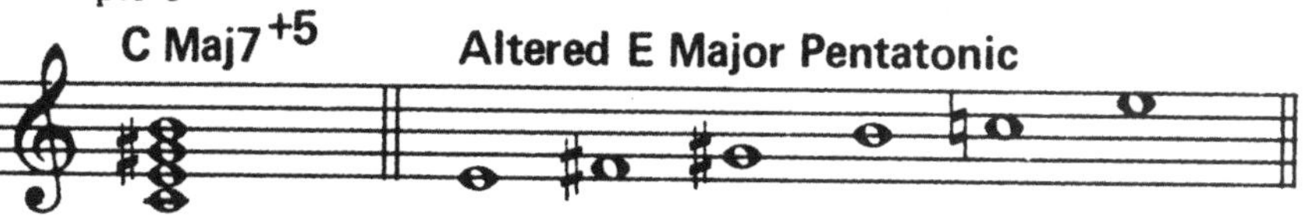


Example 6 shows the same synthetic pentatonic used in relation to an Amin♯7 chord.

Example 6

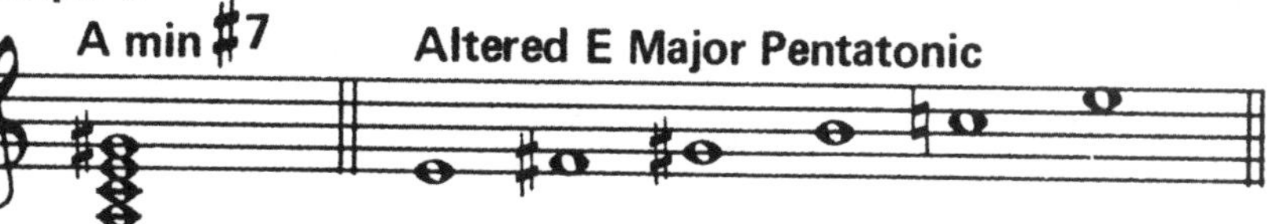


A minor 6th chord can be satisfied with one of two synthetic scales: a major pentatonic with the 3rd scale tone lowered, or a minor pentatonic with the 5th scale tone lowered. These are shown in Example 7.

Example 7

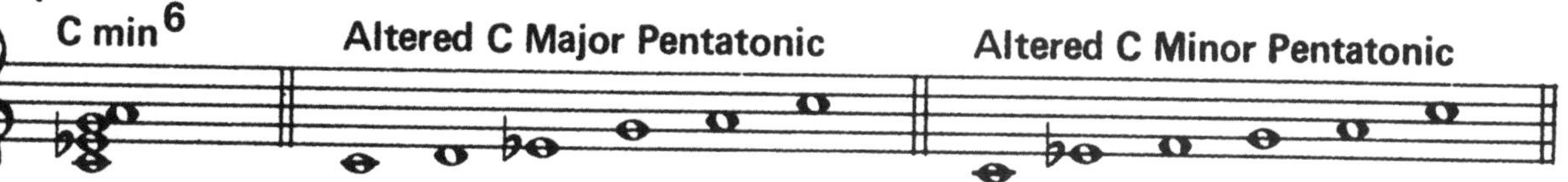


As seen in Example 8, a half-diminished chord can be handled with a minor pentatonic with the 4th scale tone lowered.

Example 8

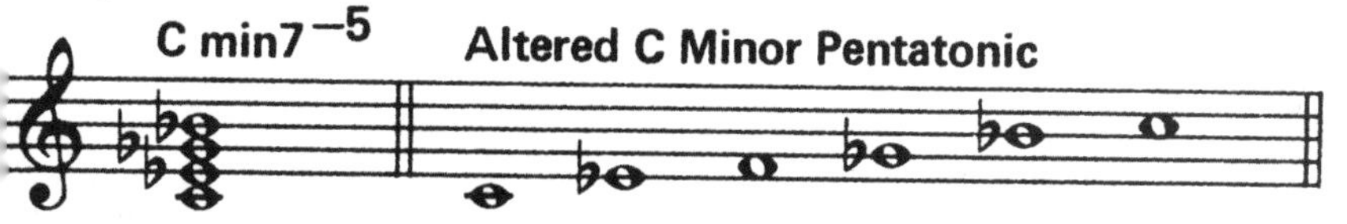


Example 9 shows the same structure used in Examples 5 and 6 related to a complete D13 chord. As before, this is an E major pentatonic with the 5th scale tone lowered.

Example 9

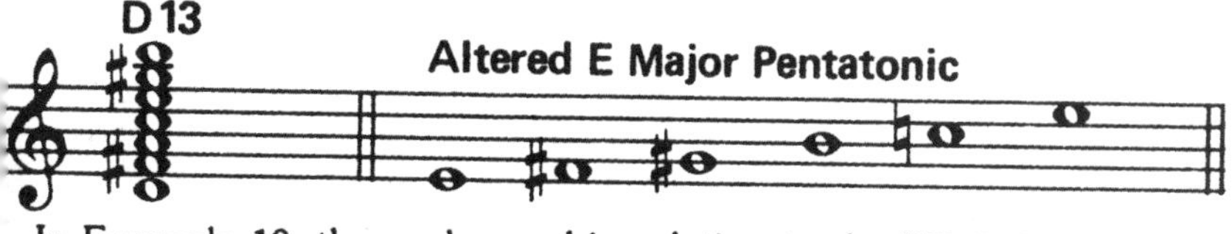


In Example 10, the scale used in relation to the B7+5+9 is a C major pentatonic with the 3rd scale tone lowered.

Example 10

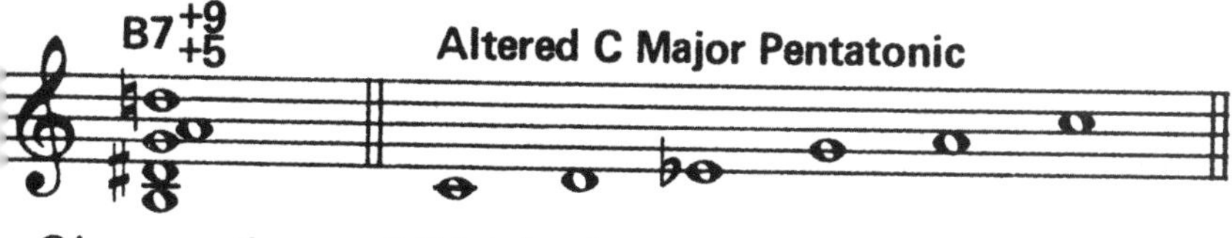


Of course, the possibilities for the creation of synthetic pentatonic scales are endless. It is hoped that these few models will stimulate experimentation and lead to the discovery of many others.

## Blues Scales

The two most commonly used blues scales are what might be called modified pentatonics, that is, pentatonic scales with the addition of a sixth scale tone. Both scales include the traditional "blue note", the lowered 3rd of the key. One also includes the lowered 5th. Notice in the following example that the first scale is a C major pentatonic with E♭ added and the second scale is a C minor pentatonic with F♯ added.

Example 11

Both of these scales can be used with dominant 7th chords. The second one can be used with minor chords as well.

Summary of Pentatonic Scale Superimpositions *

| Chord Type | Pentatonic Form | Location of Root | Chord Tones Stressed |
|---|---|---|---|
| Major | Major | Root of chord | 1, 9, 3, 5, 6(13) |
| Major | Major | 5th of chord | 5, 6, 7, 9, 3 |
| Major | Major | 9th of chord | 9, 3, +11, 13, 7 |
| Minor | Minor | Root of chord | 1, 3, 11, 5, 7 |
| Minor | Minor | 5th of chord | 5, 7, 1, 9, 11 |
| Minor | Minor | 9th of chord | 9, 11, 5, 13, 1 |
| Dominant | Major | Root of chord | 1, 9, 3, 5, 13 |
| Dom. sus4 | Major | 4th of chord | 4, 5, 6, 1, 9 |
| Dom. sus4 | Major | 7th of chord | 7, 1, 9, 4, 5 |
| Dom. +9 | Minor | Root of chord | 1, +9, 4, 5, 7 |
| Dom. +5+9 | Major | Tri-tone away | -5, +5, 7, -9, +9 |

* Synthetic pentatonics are not included.

## STUDY QUESTIONS

1. What is a pentatonic scale and where is it found on the piano?
2. Define the structure of a major pentatonic scale.
3. Define the structure of a minor pentatonic scale.
4. What is the relationship of the major and minor pentatonic forms?
5. What are synthetic pentatonic scales?
6. What are blues scales and how do they compare with pentatonics?
7. Summarize the common applications of pentatonic scales to various chord types.

## EXERCISES

Written:

1. Write out the following pentatonic scales: D major, C♯ minor, E♭ major, F minor, F♯ minor, A major, G minor, A♭ minor, B♭ minor, and B major.
2. Write out a synthetic pentatonic scale for each of the following: E♭ma7+5, Dmi♯7, B♭ mi6, Emi6, Gmi7-5, F13(+11), G7+5+9, E7+5+9, Bmi7-5, E♭mi♯7.
3. Write out the two common blues scale forms in the following keys: D, F, A♭, B♭ and B.
4. Write out a pentatonic scale for these chords: Fma13, Gma6, B♭ma9, Bmi11, Ami9, E♭mi13, D♭7, G7sus4, A7+9, E7+5+9.

Keyboard:

1. Play major and/or minor pentatonic scales in several keys. Notice that, unlike other scales, the thumb must often be used on a black note and that some scales have more than one good fingering. After playing all the tones of a particular scale in order, play it in broken fashion (1st and 3rd tones, 2nd and 4th tones. etc.). Notice that this produces many intervals of a perfect 4th. 4thy melodic patterns are characteristic of the pentatonic idiom.
2. Play a particular pentatonic scale to familiarize yourself with it. Now select at random any combination of 4 or 5 scale tones to form a chord voicing. Transpose certain scale tones up or down an octave and use both hands to play the chords you create. As you experiment, you will find some combinations that appeal to you more than others. Analyze the interval structure of these voicings and observe what chord tones are being stressed. Write your favorites down in a notebook and save them until they are thoroughly memorized.

Ear-training:

1. Sing major and minor pentatonic scales up from the root and back down again. Try singing some synthetic forms as well.
2. Working with a friend, learn to identify the specific pentatonic scale being played over a particular chord. Refer to the Summary of Pentatonic Scale Superimpositions.
3. Listen for the use of pentatonic scales on recordings. Major pentatonic on the root was used extensively during the dixieland and swing eras. Major or minor pentatonic on the 9th was used to create lydian or dorian feelings in the modal era. In the 70's, musicians superimpose major or minor pentatonics many places over the harmony and make extensive use of synthetic scales. Listen particularly to the use of pentatonics by players such as Woody Shaw, Dave Liebman, McCoy Tyner and Chick Corea.
4. Transcribe solos and analyze the use of various pentatonics. Check by playing with the recording.

## 13. FIVE PART HARMONY

Since the standard jazz band instrumentation seems to involve sections of five instruments (5 saxes, 5 trumpets, and 5 trombones), it is important to be able to voice chords in 5 parts. Several approaches to that end will be examined in this chapter: expansion of three note voicings, chords voiced in 4ths, modal harmony and polychord voicings. None of these approaches is better than the others, they simply create different musical effects.

### Expansion of Three Note Voicings

In Chapter 7, you were introduced to several 3 note voicings built on the 3rd or 7th of major, minor and dominant chords. These same voicings can provide the basis for 5 part harmony. Example 1 shows a chord progression using 3 note voicings and following the guidelines for their smooth connection explained in Chapter 7.

Example 1

D min7 G9 C Maj7 E♭Maj7 D♭Maj7 C min7 B 13 E Maj7 F9 B♭Maj7

In the next example, all that has been done is to add the root to each of the chords from Example 1 in the bass. This part would probably be played by a bass trombone or baritone sax.

Example 2

In the final example of this series, a 5th part has been added to each voicing to fill out the harmony. Generally, this part would probably be added in between the 1st and 2nd or 2nd and 3rd parts. However, depending on the key and register, it might be added between the bottom two parts. Notice that the new tone added to each chord is either an extension or alteration of the harmony to add fullness or tension.

Example 3

Though the bass part may be somewhat angular in root position harmony such as this, there is a very strong, clear sense of the harmony present at all times. This type of harmony would lend itself very well to a sax or trombone section either in a soli or as accompaniment.

## Chords Voiced in 4ths

Chords voiced in 4ths tend to have a light open quality about them. However, a chord does not have to be built only in 4ths nor does it have to be built exclusively of perfect 4ths to fit this category. As long as the majority of intervals in the voicing are perfect 4ths, the chord will have this general flavor about it. The following example shows some typical 4thy voicings that could be used with C major, C minor and C dominant 7th chords.

Example 4

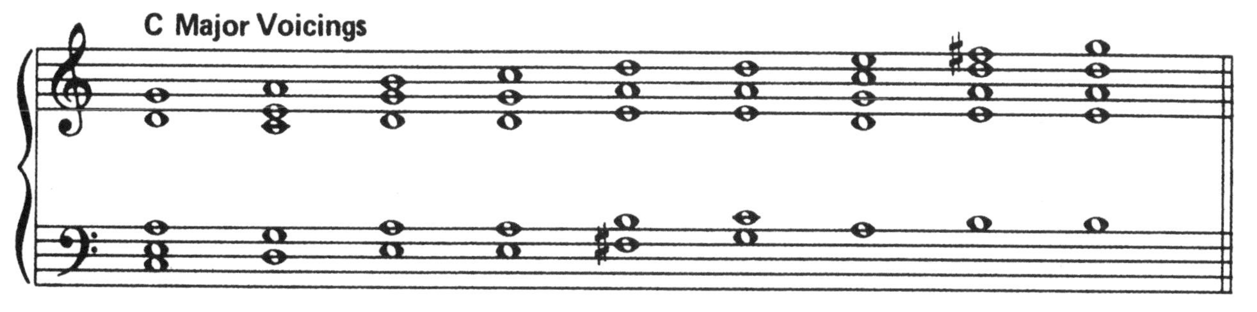


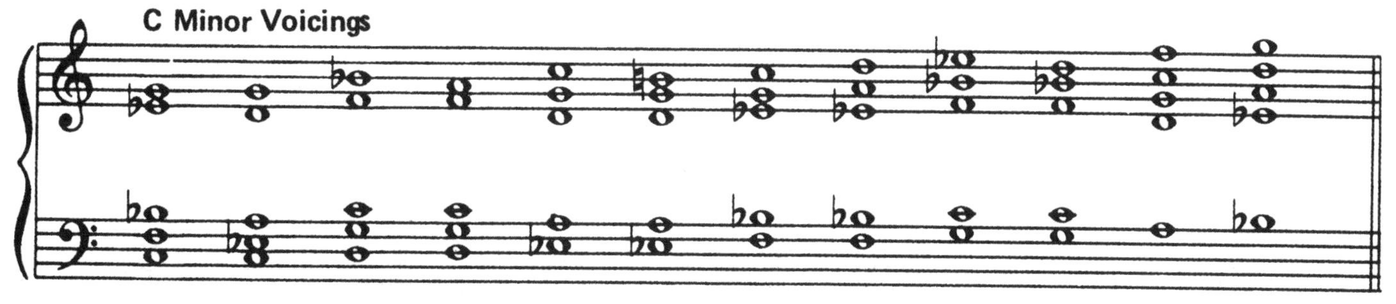


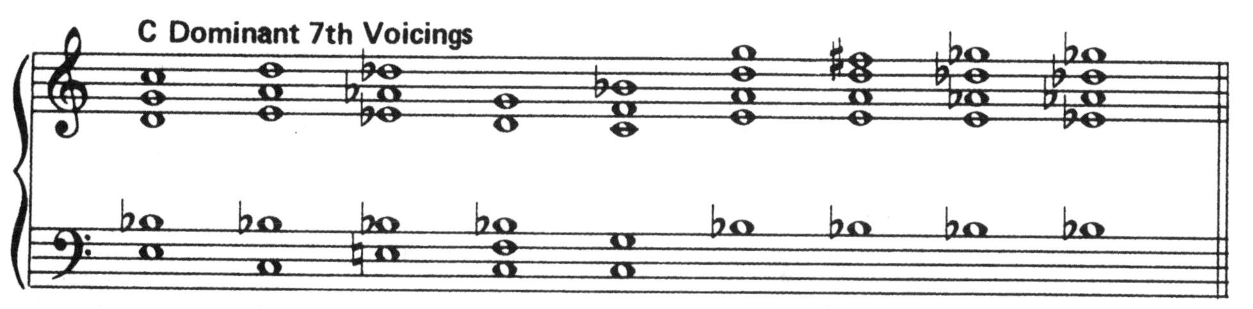


There are some observations that can be made about 4thy voicings that may help develop an overall way of thinking about them:

1) A major 3rd, major 7th or +11 on top of a voicing tends to result in a bright sounding chord. This is also true of the presence of a major 3rd interval between the top two notes of the chord.

2) If the bottom note of the voicing is the root of the chord, the voicing seems stronger; if the root is not the bottom note, the voicing seems lighter.

3) A consonant interval such as a major 3rd on the bottom of the voicing adds to the clarity; a dissonant interval such as a major 7th tends to obscure the harmony.

4) Generally speaking, voicings which combine two or more perfect 4ths with a major 3rd tend to sound the best.

## Modal Harmony

If a particular mode is assigned to a harmony, it can then generate chords that obviously relate to the sound. Modal voicings may also be 4thy in their spacing but do not have to be. Example 5 shows a C major chord which has been assigned a lydian scale. The voicings that follow are a more or less random selection of tones from the C Lydian scale.

Example 5

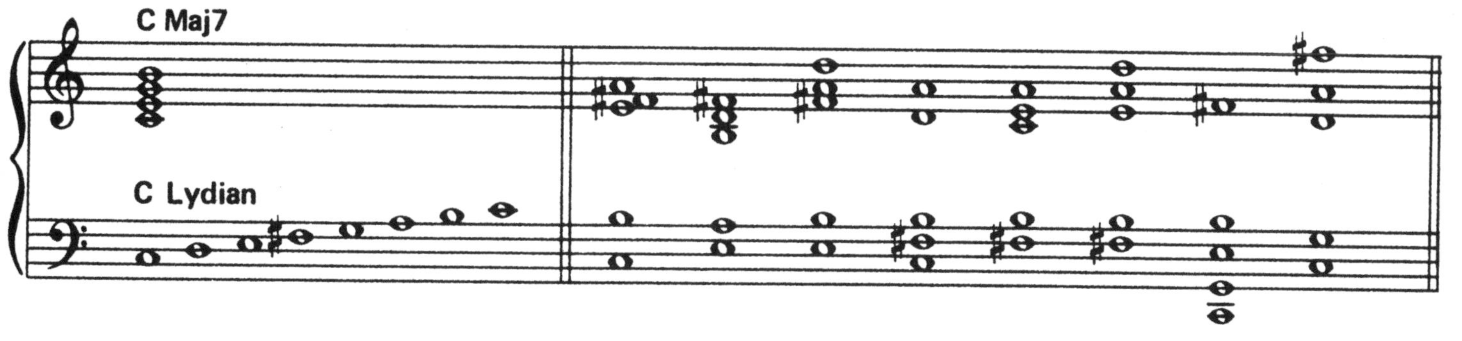


Notice in the previous example that some voicings are more consonant and some are more dissonant. The choice would depend on the musical effect desired. Also, each of the voicings has the +11 (raised 4th) scale step which is characteristic of a lydian mode.

The next example shows a minor chord which has been assigned a dorian sound. As before, the characteristic tone of the mode (the raised 6th) has been included in each voicing.

Example 6

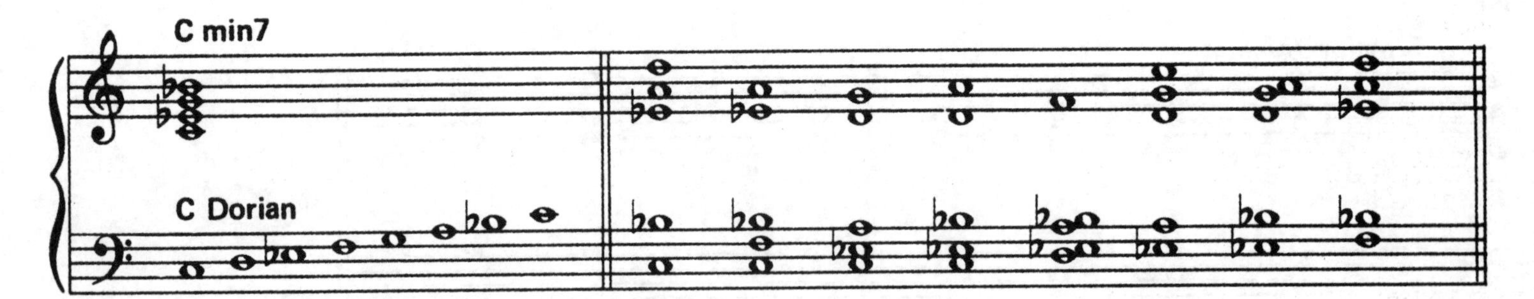


The same concept can be applied to any scale whether it is actually called a mode or not. For example, in the following example, a half step-whole step diminished scale has been assigned to a dominant 7th chord. In this case, the characteristic tones are the altered 9ths and the natural 13th.

Example 7

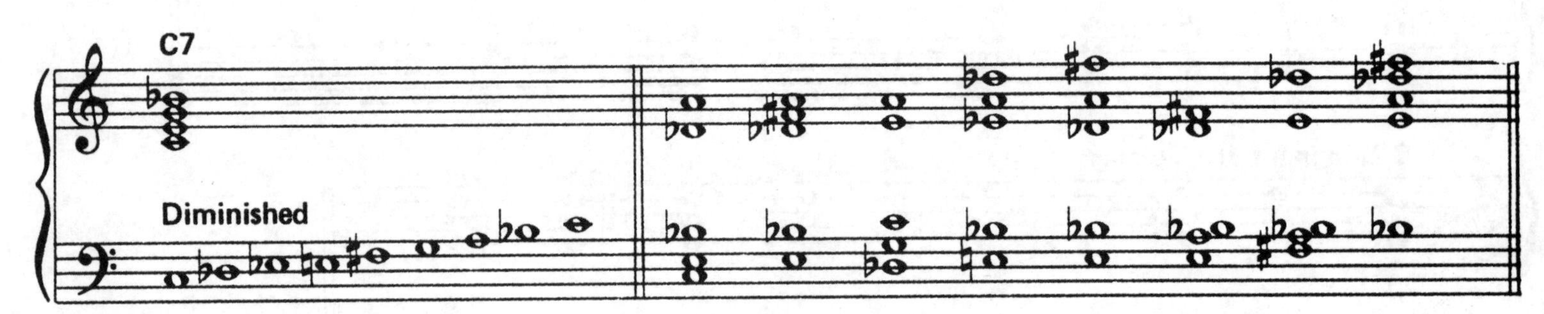


Taking this idea a step further, one could create synthetic scales (to be studied in the last chapter) and let them in turn generate their own series of chords. Through trial and error, one eventually becomes very selective about modal voicings just as he has favorite conventional voicings. The interval structure of the voicing and the particular chord tones included both have a big effect on the final result. But at first, a certain amount of random experimentation will lead to the discovery of some interesting possibilities!

## Polychord Voicings

In Chapter 9, polychord nomenclature was shown to be an easy way to quickly arrive at complex sounds. However, nothing was said about voicing chords at that time.

Basically, to voice chords so that they really sound like a polychord, one has only to keep the two parts of the polychord separate from each other. Example 8 shows two arrangements of the same six tones: the first does not sound like a polychord because the tones of the two triads have been intermingled.

Example 8

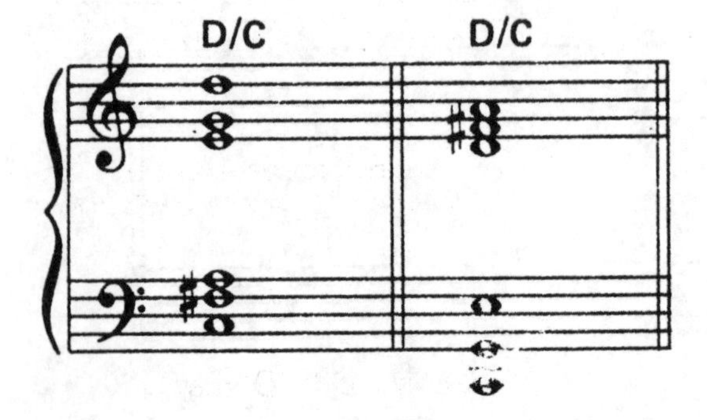


In the second of the two voicings above, the two triads have been kept separate from each other so it is possible to actually hear them as two chords or a polychord!

In voicing polychords in 5 parts, it is obvious that some choices have to be made as to which 5 tones to include or omit. Remember that important color tones such as 3rds, 7ths and altered tones should probably be included. The root of the bottom chord, which may be sounded elsewhere, and an unaltered 5th may be left out. Also, if the upper triad of the polychord includes one of the essential color tones of the bottom chord, then it need not be included in the bottom chord. Example 9 shows some 5 part polychord voicings that relate to all 5 types of 7th chords.

Example 9

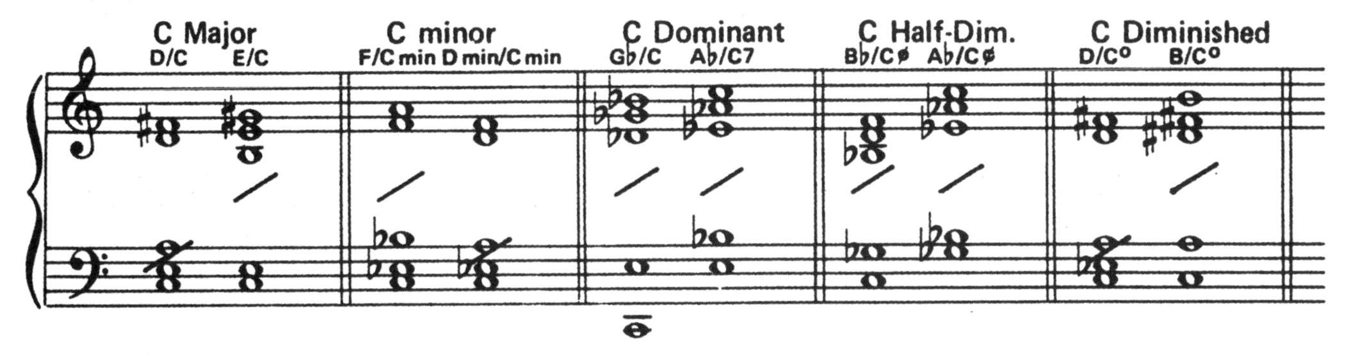


Notice in the previous example that the half-diminished chord voicing includes the 5th which is an important color tone. The fully diminished 7th chord only requires the interval of the diminished 7th between the root and 7th to identify itself.

One overall principle of voicing should be mentioned. There should generally always be an interval of a minor 3rd or larger between the top two tones of any voicing to avoid a possible conflict between the 2nd part and the melody.

## STUDY QUESTIONS

1. How do you expand a 3 note voicing into a 5 part chord?
2. What is required to create a voicing which has a 4thy sound?
3. What factors seem to affect the quality of 4thy voicings?
4. What is the principle behind a modal approach to voicing chords?
5. What insures that a polychord sounds like a polychord?
6. What considerations should be kept in mind when selecting chord tones for a 5 part polychord voicing?
7. What overall principle of voicing should be kept in mind?

## EXERCISES

Written:

1. Expand the following progression into 5 part harmony by adding the root of each chord in the bass and a 5th part in between the original 3 parts.

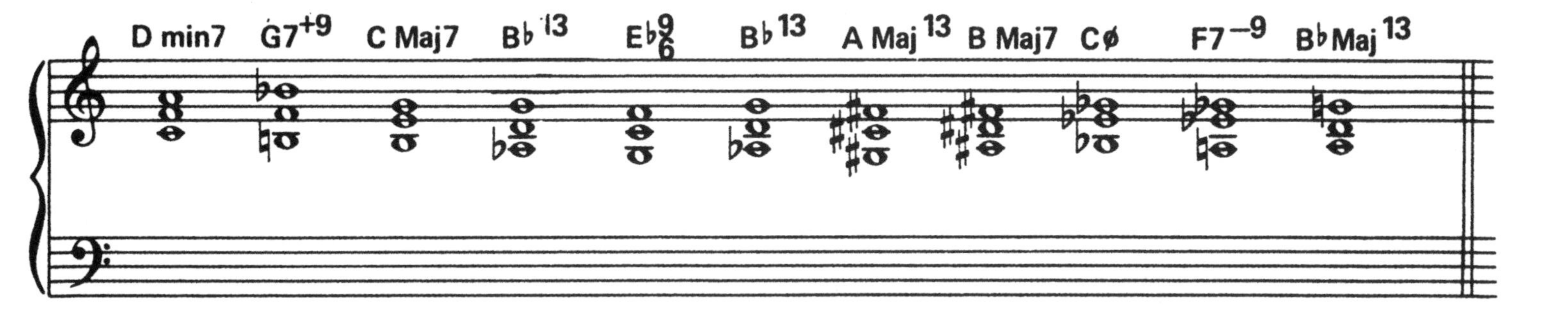


2. Voice the following progressions in 5 parts by following these 3 steps: 1) Choose three note voicings for each chord being sure to connect them smoothly, 2) Add the root as a bass note for each chord, and 3) Add the 5th part to each chord making sure that it connects smoothly as well.

   a) E♭ma7 Cmi7 Fmi7 B♭7 Bmi7 E7 Fmi7 B♭7 Gmi7 G♭ma7 Emi7 A7 Dma7

   b) Cmi7 A♭ma7 Dmi7-5 G7-9 E♭ma7 Fmi7 G7+9 Cmi7 Dmi7-5 G7-9 Cmi7.

   c)Gma7 Cma7 Ami7 D7 E♭ma7 A♭7 Gma7 Bmi7 Cmi7 F7 Gma7 E7+9 Ami7 D7 D♭ma7.

3. Voice the following progression in 5 parts using voicings that are mainly composed of perfect 4ths. Use only inversions that do not have the root on the bottom:

   Fma7 Gmi7 A♭ma7 D♭ma7 Dmi7 G7 Cmi7 F7 B♭ma7 Ami7 Gmi7 C7 Fma7

4. Harmonize the following modal melodies using only scale tones suggested by the modal key signature.

5. Voice the following polychords in 5 parts:
D/C, G/B♭7, A♭ /F, G/E♭ bass, Ami7/D bass, B♭/D7, F/Cmi, C/Fmi A/E♭, Ami/Gmi.

Keyboard:

1. Working from lead sheets which include only chord symbols, try to play 5 part harmony at sight. Play only roots of chords in the left hand and 4 parts in the right hand. Be sure that the right hand has either the 3rd or 7th of each chord as the bottom part of the 4.
2. Pick a particular type of chord in a certain key and play all of the 4thy voicings that you can find for that one chord. Keep repeating this process with different types of chords in other keys. Write down favorites in a note book to be memorized later.
3. Pick a particular mode (or any type of scale) in a given key. Try to visualize that scale all the way up and down the keyboard so strongly that the other keys seem to disappear from the piano. Now begin to randomly select tones from the scale to create 5 note voicings. Play 2 tones in one hand and 3 in the other. Repeat this procedure with other scales in other keys.
4. Play polychord voicings in 5 parts, again playing 2 notes in one hand and 3 in the other. Work with 1 chord type in a given key and try to find all of the polychord voicings that could relate to that basic family. It may be helpful to review Chapter 9 for the various formulas.

Ear-Training:

1. Working with another person, try to learn to identify specific kinds of voicings that relate to the various chord types. Listen for the clusterish sound of 3 note voicings that have been filled in, 4thy structures, modal sounds and polychords.
2. Transcribe 5 part harmony played by saxes, trumpets or trombones on jazz band recordings. Listen for each part separately if necessary. Try to compare your "record copy" with a score if there is one available.
3. Try to sing all of the tones in various kinds of voicings from the bottom note up and back down again. This may require the use of falsetto to cover the range of the voicing. Play the voicing on the piano to help you learn to hear it.

## 14. SYNTHETIC SCALES

In addition to the conventional groups of modes and other scales commonly used by jazz musicians, there is a vast group of scales that cannot be described in usual terms. Basically, one can create a scale with any combination of tones and any arrangement of intervals in its structure. Generally, the interval structure of any scale is relatively even, that is, it divides the octave fairly evenly. For example, in a pentatonic scale there are five scale tones and the intervals between those tones are either major 2nds or minor 3rds. A major scale has seven scale tones and the intervals between those tones are either major 2nds or minor 2nds. A whole tone scale has six scale tones and includes only major 2nds between scale tones.

Synthetic scales would probably not have fewer than five tones since four tones, which divide the octave fairly evenly, would tend to create a chord arpeggiation rather than a scale. On the other hand, they would probably not have more than ten tones since they would begin to lose their identity to excessive chromaticism. Most synthetic scales that have any real practical application generally include between five and nine tones.

### The Harmonic Major

The harmonic major is a synthetic scale that is really a hybrid composed of the first half of a major scale and the second half of a harmonic minor scale. This combination results in an interesting sounding scale that, obviously, has both major and minor feelings to it. Actually, it is the reverse of the ascending melodic minor scale which is composed of the first half of a minor scale and the 2nd half of a major scale. Example 1 shows both of these scales.

Example 1

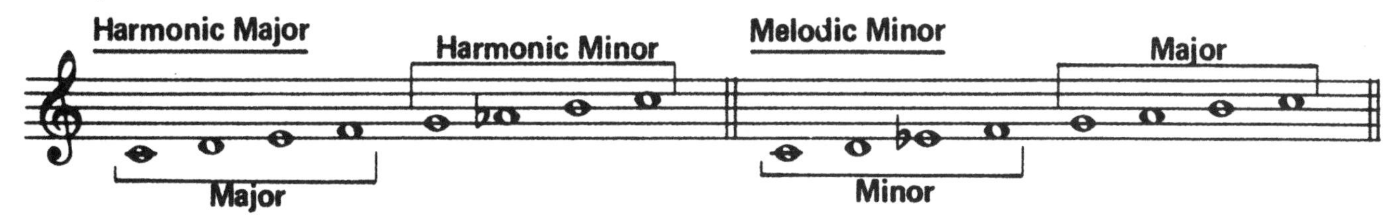


Notice in the previous example that the two scales really have a similar feeling when played. Though the melodic minor was used extensively in traditional music, the harmonic major remains a less common synthetic scale.

Once a synthetic scale such as the harmonic major is created, it can generate its own set of modes which may have useful application just as the modes of the major scale do. Example 2 shows all seven modes of the harmonic major built on the note C. The augmented second which is characteristic of both this scale and the harmonic minor is indicated in each mode.

Example 2

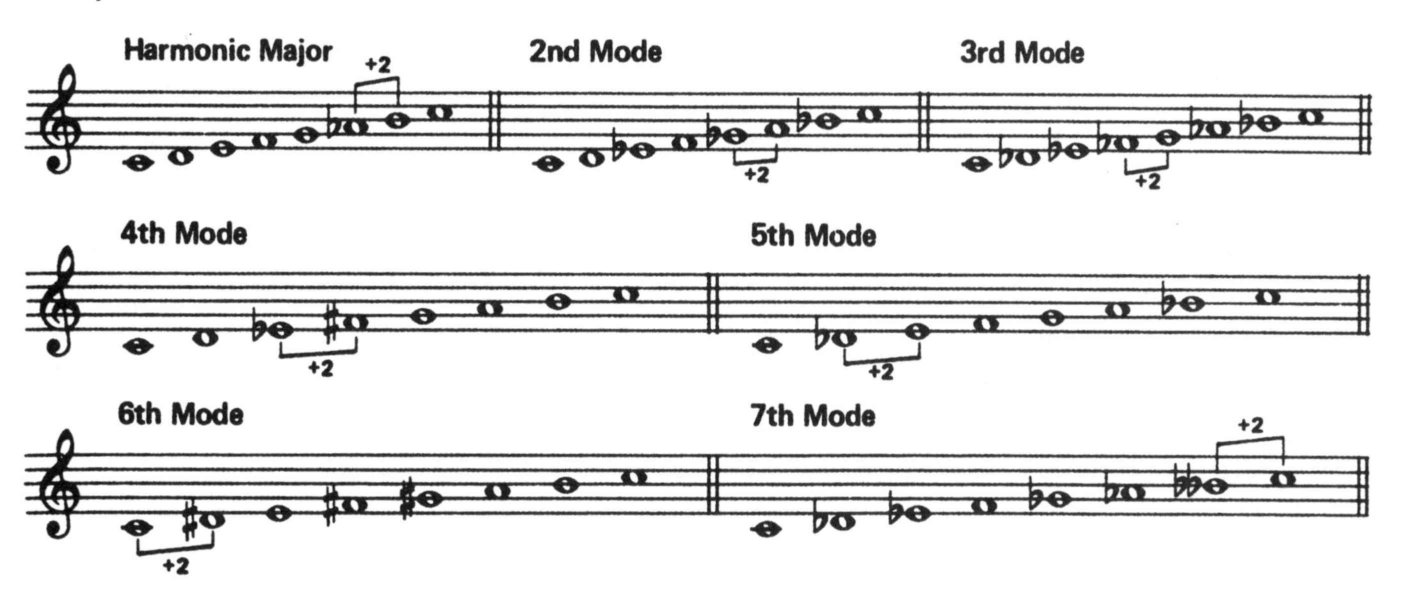


From the previous example, it should become apparent that this set of modes contributes some additional resources for handling certain seventh chord sounds. The following chart summarizes the chord-scale relationships of these scales.

| Mode of the Harmonic Major | Related 7th Chord |
|---|---|
| 1st mode | maj7 or Maj7+5 |
| 2nd mode | min7-5 |
| 3rd mode | dom7-9-13 |
| 4th mode | min♯7 |
| 5th mode | dom7-9 |
| 6th mode | maj7+5 |
| 7th mode | dim7 |

## Wrong Note Scales

Though it is not necessary to create entire groups of synthetic scales such as the modes of the harmonic major, it may often be helpful to create a single synthetic scale to fit a specific need. For example, by simply putting one wrong note in a normal scale, some unusual effects can be created. The following example shows some conventional scales with one altered or wrong note in each.

Example 3

Generally, synthetic scales will probably be less useful than the normal modes which predominate in the jazz idiom. However, in a more adventuresome approach to writing and performance, they may be very useful. In regard to the latter, it may be desirable to create a synthetic tonality as the basis for an entire composition or improvisation. This tonality would be created by a single synthetic scale which would then generate its own set of diatonic chords (sonorities which might defy being labeled). The following example shows an improvisation in a synthetic tonality which could only be called C-ish!

Example 4

Finally, in the medium of electronic synthesis, by controlling gate voltages, one can create scales with more than twelve tones and which involve intervals smaller than a half step. Twenty-four tone scales of exact quarter tones could be used or microtonal scales of anywhere between thirteen and say one hundred tones to the octave! Most musicians have difficulty singing quarter tones or smaller but many listeners are capable of appreciating the unusual musical effects created by electronic synthesis of microtonal scales.

## STUDY QUESTIONS

1. How many scale tones do synthetic scales usually have? Why?
2. What is usually true of the interval structure of synthetic scales?
3. What is the harmonic major scale? Why is it so named?
4. Why is the harmonic major a useful synthetic scale?
5. What is a wrong note scale?
6. What is a synthetic tonality?
7. What possibilities does the electronic synthesis of sound provide for the creation of scales?

## EXERCISES

Written:

1. Write out all seven modes of E♭ harmonic major.
2. Write out all seven modes of the harmonic major built on G.
3. Write a 4 or 8 measure melody in each mode of the harmonic major.
4. Create a wrong note scale from each mode of the major scale.
5. Create synthetic scales of 8, 9, and 10 tones.

Keyboard:

1. Play synthetic scales at the piano to make it easier to visualize their structures.
2. Create a synthetic scale and see how many diatonic chords you can create using spacings of 2nds, 3rds and 4ths.

Ear-Training:

1. Listen for the use of synthetic scales by adventuresome improvisers on recordings. Transcribe specific scales and analyze their relationships to the chords which they accompany.
2. Sing synthetic scales as an exercise in intervals. Play an appropriate chord along with each scale as you sing it and then sing without the chord.
3. Listen to electronic music involving microtones. Try to perceive how many tones are involved and identify them as closely as possible.

# APPENDIX I

## DEVELOPING IMPROVISATIONAL SKILLS

### How to Practice

1. Practice with a metronome.
   A. Use it as record of progress by keeping track of the most recent tempos at which you practice various problems.
   B. Use it to determine the evenness of running notes by setting it to "click" at the speed of various subdivisions of the beat such as triplets or sixteenth notes.
   C. Use it as an aid to gradually increasing the speed of technical passages.
   D. Use it to improve your time by having it "click" on various beats of the measure; for example, in 4/4 time, try setting it to beat all four beats, or just 1 and 3, or 2 and 4, or only the first beat of the bar, or in 3/4 set it for 2 against 3 (1 and the end of 2).
   E. Use it in all of your practice session: literature, technique, scales and arpeggios, improvisation, etc.
2. Practice slowly! Only play something as fast as you can play it perfectly every time even if that means 1/4 tempo or 1/10 tempo. Then after satisfying yourself that you can play the problem, move the metronome up one notch at a time until you reach a particular tempo-goal. Be patient!
3. Practice over the entire range of your instrument.
4. Practice scales, patterns, motives, etc., *in all keys*!
5. Budget your practice time to include all of the following: technical etudes, scales and arpeggios, patterns, melodic fragments, keyboard harmony, tune learning, etc.
6. Practice regularly! Develop a practice routine and don't ever break it. That means practicing at the same time and place every day. Practicing 1 hour a day, *every day*, is far superior to practicing 7 hours once a week.
7. Practice as much as you can but it may be necessary to pace yourself. For example, you can rest your lip while practicing keyboard harmony or singing intervals. Or you may want to spread your practice over 2 or 3 sessions during different periods of the day or night.
8. Practice at least 2 hours a day but spend as much time as you need to on various parts of your practice session. For instance, you may require 20 minutes for warm-up, 30 minutes for scales, 45 minutes for etudes, 45 minutes for patterns, etc.
9. Tape record your practice sessions occasionally. This will help you see your progress as well as allowing you to be objectively critical of things that still need work. Don't do it too often or the small amount of progress may be discouraging. Just remember that, if you practice *correctly* and *patiently*, improvement is taking place!

### What to Practice

1. Devote serious attention to classical literature on your instrument. Every new piece you play presents technical problems which, when conquered, will help you gain more control of your instrument, thus more ease in improvising.
2. Practice technical etudes which focus attention on a limited number of special problems.
3. Practice scales: all types, all keys, in different rhythmic values and groupings, over the full range of your instrument. Pianists practice hands separately at first and then hands together.
4. Work for good, correct tone production (in the classical sense) so that you can play in tune, with a good sound and clean articulation.
5. Practice stylistic devices peculiar to jazz such as vibrato, tone effects, note-bending, jazz phrasing, etc.
6. Practice various types of melodic patterns in all keys. Work out original ideas on certain chord progressions and learn them in all keys.
7. Devote some time to learning tunes. Set goals for yourself and try to learn so many tunes each week. This means being able to play the melody and improvise on the chord progression without the music. Play the chord progression at the keyboard.
8. "Woodshed" tunes by really zeroing in on any chords of the progression which may be troublesome to you. Make sure you have carefully analyzed chord-scale relationships and can play all of the pertinent scales smoothly and effortlessly. Play the chords at the keyboard.
9. Practice improvising with the metronome as your rhythm section. As in dealing with technical problems, start with slower tempos on difficult tunes and gradually increase them.
10. Though it isn't officially part of your practice session, you should listen to as much music of all kinds as possible and apply the insights you gain during your practice session.

# APPENDIX II

## MELODY HARMONIZATION CHECK-LIST

When choosing each successive chord in the harmonization of a melody, consider the following points:

1. Will the bass note (root?) of that chord contribute to a melodic flow in the bass line?
2. Can the melody tone be accounted for as a chord tone or an alteration in the chord chosen for it?
3. Is the quality (Maj., min., dom.) of the chord appropriate to follow the previous chord?
4. Is the progression desired strong (down a half step, down a 5th), moderate (down a whole step, down a 3rd, up a 5th), or weak (up a half step, up a whole step, up a 3rd)?
5. When writing for particular instruments (baritone sax, bass trombone, bass clarinet, tuba), is the bass note chosen within the range of the instrument?
6. Is there too much repetition of certain chord roots which produces harmonic monotony?

## CHORD VOICING CHECK-LIST

After a particular chord has been selected for a harmonic progression, observe the following points:

1. Chord should be spelled correctly with all necessary chromatic alterations present.
2. The spacing between chord tones should be relatively even with the exception of the bottom two tones.
3. Unless omitted for a special reason, the root, 3rd and 7th should be present in the chord.
4. In 5-part harmony, five different chord tones should be used unless a 7th chord is desired, in which case the 3rd, 5th or 7th is usually doubled.
5. In connecting two chords, the voice-leading of each individual inner part (melody and bass excepted) should be a smooth melodic motion, preferably a perfect 4th or less.
6. In handling relationships such as the root to Maj. 7th, 3rd to (+)9th, 5th to +11th, min. 7th to 13th, the lower chord tone of the two should normally be below the other or else a half step away from it.
7. The bottom interval of the chord should outline the fundamental quality (M. or m. 3rd, p. 5th, M. or m. 7th, M. or m. 10th).
8. Avoid placing the 2nd part either a half or whole step from melody.

# APPENDIX III

## HINTS ON TRANSCRIBING SOLOS

1. USE A TAPE RECORDER.
   - A. reel-to-reel recorder - dub the solo from the original recording using the high speed of the recorder. Then you have the option of listening to the solo at its true speed or, switching to the slow speed of the recorder, at half speed to facilitate hearing fast passages. At the slow speed, all the notes will sound an octave lower than the original so don't forget to write them an octave higher.
   - B. cassette recorder - cassette decks or portable players are more convenient to carry to the piano or to a practice room to work on the solo. However, they only play at one speed so, in dubbing the solo to cassette, a reel-to-reel recorder or a phonograph with a 16 rpm speed will be needed to produce the half-speed version of the solo. Both the original speed and half-speed version of the solo should be recorded on the cassette as both serve different purposes in transcribing a solo.
2. SECURE AN ACCURATE SET OF CHORD CHANGES FOR THE SOLO.
   - A. lead sheet available - the tune may be a standard or popular jazz tune that is already known to you or is readily found in fake books or anthologies. However, it is still a good idea to double check the progression to make sure there are no unusual substitutions or that the lead sheet is accurate.
   - B. transcribing the chord progression - very often it will be necessary to transcribe the chord progression because it is not known to you and is not available in any books. First, ascertain the form of the tune and sketch the large sections out on manuscript paper, placing double bars at the beginning of each section. Then, listening to bass for roots and the piano or guitar for chord quality, write in the chords. The bass may not always play roots of chords but most of the time the root will be sounded at or near the beginning of each new chord change. Also, listen for common functions like II-V-I.
3. PROCEDURE FOR TRANSCRIBING THE SOLO.
   - A. analyze chord-scale relationships to narrow down the choices to listen for when scale motion is involved.
   - B. work in pencil to make correction easier. A number 2 lead is easy to read and erase. The final copy may be in ink.
   - C. begin by listening only for pitches. Write them down on the staff as quarter notes (heads only, no stems) and omit bar lines.
   - D. locate bar lines - after all pitches have been transcribed, go through and locate which notes fall on or right after the first beats of measures. Place bar lines in front of them.
   - E. locate other beats in the measure - same process as step D.
   - F. analyze rhythmic patterns - examine each group of notes within any given beat. Add stems and beams, any rests required.
4. ALTERNATE BETWEEN ORIGINAL AND HALF-SPEED VERSIONS
   - A. original speed - usually better for checking rhythms, articulation and even pitches if range is low and muddy at slow speed.
   - B. half-speed - usually necessary for fast passages. Listen for one additional note on each hearing in some cases.
5. USE BOTH PLAYING AND SINGING TO TEST WHAT YOU ARE HEARING.

## APPENDIX IV

## MODE IDENTIFICATION GUIDE

I. If you hear a *major 3rd*:
- A. If you hear a *lowered 2nd*:
  - 1) If you hear a *perfect 5th*:
    - 5th Mode Harmonic Minor (♭6)
    - Half-Whole Diminished (nat. 6)
  - 2) If you hear a *lowered 5th*:
    - Super Locrian
- B. If you hear a *natural 2nd*:
  - 1) If you hear a *natural 4th*:
    - Major
    - Mixolydian (♭7)
    - 3rd Mode Harmonic Minor (♯5)
    - Mixolydian, ♭6, (♭6, ♭7)
  - 2) If you hear a *raised 4th*:
    - Lydian
    - Lydian, ♭7 (♭7)
    - Lydian-Augmented (♯5)
    - Whole Tone (♯5, ♭7)

II. If you hear a *minor 3rd*:
- A. If you hear a *lowered 2nd*:
  - 1) If you hear a *perfect 5th*:
    - Phrygian (♭6)
    - Dorian, ♭2 (nat. 6)
  - 2) If you hear a *lowered 5th*:
    - Locrian
    - 2nd Mode Harmonic Minor (♯6)
    - 7th Mode Harmonic Minor (♭4, ♭7)
- B. If you hear a *natural 2nd*:
  - 1) If you hear a *perfect 5th*:
    - Dorian (nat. 6)
    - Melodic Minor (nat. 6 & 7)
    - Aeolian (♭6)
    - 4th Mode Harmonic Minor (♯4)
  - 2) If you hear a *lowered 5th*:
    - Locrian, ♯2
    - Whole-Half Diminished (♭7, nat. 7)

III. If you hear a *major 3rd* and a *minor 3rd* with *no 2nd*:
- Augmented (♯5)
- 6th Mode Harmonic Minor (nat. 5)

## APPENDIX V

## A SUGGESTED COURSE SYLLABUS

The Jazz Language is used by the author as a text for a two-semester jazz theory course which he teaches at North Texas State University. This course, which is called Jazz Fundamentals, is required of all jazz majors. Even though the course is taken concurrently with the study of traditional harmony, it is aimed primarily at freshmen and, accordingly, must allow for a certain lack of background on the part of many students. The following is a summary of grading policies and outlines of both semesters of the course.

### MUSIC 136-137, JAZZ FUNDAMENTALS - GRADING POLICY

Successful completion of Music 136-137 with grades of A or B is a prerequisite for both Jazz Improvisation and Jazz Arranging. The purpose of this syllabus is to maintain consistent teaching standards through all sections and to inform students of their responsibilities for successful progress through and completion of the course.

Grading is based primarily on three 50-minute examinations and one 2-hour final examination each semester. These are spaced evenly throughout the semesters and the weekly outlines indicate the location of each test as well as the material covered. Roughly speaking, the formula for computing the semester grade is as follows:

| | |
|---|---|
| 1st Quarter Examination | - 20% |
| Mid-term examination | - 20% |
| 3rd Quarter Examination | - 20% |
| Final Examination | - 40% |
| Total | 100% |

Homework may or may not affect the final grade depending on the size of the class, attendance and performance on examinations.

Dictation quizzes will be averaged and will have some impact on the determination of the semester grade, especially in borderline cases. These quizzes may not be made up except in instances where an excused absence is involved.

### MUSIC 136, JAZZ FUNDAMENTALS - SEMESTER OUTLINE

| WEEK | 1ST CLASS PERIOD | 2ND CLASS PERIOD |
|---|---|---|
| 1 | Lecture: Orientation | Lecture: Intervals |
| 2 | Drill: Interval spelling and ear-training | Homework: Ch. 1, exercises 1-4<br>Drill: Spelling and ear-training |
| 3 | Lecture: Basic Chord construction | Dictation quiz: Intervals<br>Drill: Chord spelling, ear-training |
| 4 | Homework: Ch. 2, exercises 1-4<br>Drill: Spelling and ear-training | 1st Quarter Examination (50 minutes)<br>Covers material in chapters 1 & 2. |
| 5 | Lecture: Modes of the major scale | Dictation Quiz: Seventh chords<br>Drill: Mode spelling, ear-training |
| 6 | Homework: Ch. 3, exercises 1-3<br>Drill: Spelling and ear-training | Lecture: Substitution and function |
| 7 | Dictation quiz: Major modes<br>Drill: Substitution and function | Homework: Ch. 4, Exercises 1 & 2<br>Drill: Substitution and function |
| 8 | Dictation quiz: Common functions<br>Homework: Ch. 4, Exercises 3 & 4 | Mid-term Examination (50 minutes)<br>Covers material in chapters 1-4. |
| 9 | Lecture: 13th chords | Drill: 13th chord spelling and ear-training |
| 10 | Homework: Ch. 5, exercises 1-3<br>Drill: Spelling and ear-training | Lecture: Harmonic minor modes |
| 11 | Dictation quiz: 13th chords<br>Drill: Mode spelling, ear-training | Homework: Ch. 6, Exercises 1-3<br>Drill: Spelling and ear-training |
| 12 | Dictation quiz: Harmonic minor<br>Drill: Spelling and ear-training | 3rd Quarter Examination (50 minutes)<br>Covers material in chapters 5 & 6 |
| 13 | Lecture: Chord voicing, connection | Drill: Voicing spelling |
| 14 | Homework: Ch. 7, Exercises 1-4<br>Drill: Voicing connection | Homework: Ch. 7, Exercise 5a<br>Drill: Voicing connection |
| 15 | Homework: Ch. 7, Exercises 5b, 5c<br>Drill: Voicing connection | Review: Chapters 1-7 |

Final Examination (120 minutes): Scheduled during final exam week. Covers material in chapters 1-7.

## MUSIC 137, JAZZ FUNDAMENTALS - SEMESTER OUTLINE

| WEEK | 1ST CLASS PERIOD | 2ND CLASS PERIOD |
|---|---|---|
| 1 | Lecture: Orientation and review of Music 136 | Lecture: Melodic minor modes |
| 2 | Drill: Mode spelling and ear-training | Homework: Ch. 8, Exercises 1-3<br>Drill: Spelling and ear-training |
| 3 | Lecture: Polychord nomenclature | Dictation quiz: Melodic minor modes<br>Drill: Polychords, ear-training |
| 4 | Homework: Ch. 9, Exercises 1-3<br>Drill: Polychords, ear-training | 1st Quarter Examination (50 minutes)<br>Covers material in Chapters 8 & 9 |
| 5 | Dictation quiz: Polychords<br>Lecture: Sym. Altered Scales | Drill: Sym. Altered scales,<br>spelling and ear-training |
| 6 | Homework: Ch. 10, Exercises 1-4<br>Drill: Spelling and ear-training | Lecture: Advanced function<br>and substitution |
| 7 | Dictation quiz: Altered scales<br>Drill: Function, substitution | Homework: Ch. 11, Exercise 1a<br>Drill: Function, substitution |
| 8 | Homework: Ch. 11, Exercises 1b & c<br>Drill: Function, substitution | Mid-term Examination (50 minutes)<br>Covers material in Chapters 8-11 |
| 9 | Lecture: Pentatonic scales | Drill: Pentatonic scales,<br>spelling and ear-training |
| 10 | Homework: Ch. 12, Exercises 1 & 2<br>Drill: Spelling and ear-training | Homework: Ch. 12, Exercises 3 & 4<br>Dictation Quiz: Pentatonic scales |
| 11 | Lecture: Five part harmony | Drill: Five part harmony |
| 12 | Homework: Ch. 13, Exercises 1 & 2<br>Drill: Five part harmony | 3rd Quarter Examination (50 minutes)<br>Covers material in Chapters 12 & 13 |
| 13 | Homework: Ch. 13, Exercise 3<br>Drill: Five part harmony | Homework: Ch. 13, Exercise 5<br>Drill: Five part harmony |
| 14 | Lecture: Synthetic scales | Drill: Harmonic major modes,<br>spelling and ear-training |
| 15 | Homework: Ch. 14, Exercises 1 & 2<br>Drill: Synthetic scales | Review: Chapters 8-14 |

Final Examination (120 minutes): Scheduled during final exam week. Covers material in Chapters 8-14